The Cocker Spaniel

A Vet's Guide on How To Care For Your Cocker Spaniel Dog

WRITTEN BY

DR. GORDON ROBERTS BVSC MRCVS

Hello! My name is Gordon Roberts and I'm the author of this book. I hope you enjoy all of the specialist advice it contains. I'm a huge advocate of preventative care for animals, and I'd love to see more pet owners taking the time to research their pet's health care needs.

Being proactive and educating yourself about your pet's health now, rather than later on, could save you and your pet a lot of trouble in the long run.

If you'd like to read more of my professional pet care advice simply go to my website at http://drgordonroberts.com/freereportsdownload/.

As a thank you for purchasing this book, you'll find dozens of bonus pet care reports there to download and keep, absolutely free of charge!

Best wishes,

Gordon

Founder, Wellpets

Contents

Breed Profile

Introduction

The English Cocker Spaniel is among the oldest Spaniel breeds and are descendants of Spain's original Spaniels. The breed was first used as a hunting dog. It received official recognition by the American Kennel Club in 1946. Today, Cockers are seldom used for hunting. They have evolved to become great pets for many households.

English Cocker Spaniels are medium-sized dogs with long and feathered ears. They have a compact and athletic body frame, a proportionate head, flared nostrils and a strong, square muzzle. Cockers may have docked tails, but only if considered to be working dogs and certified by a registered vet, have straight forelegs and hind legs that are angulated. They have a medium-length silky coat which can either be flat or slightly wavy. The breed comes in various coat colours including solid black, liver or red markings, parti-coloured or roan. Two types or lines of English Cocker Spaniels have been identified—field and show. Show type Cockers possess longer coats than field types.

History

The Cocker Spaniel is descended from the original Spaniels of Spain, which went on to become a very diverse breed in terms of size, colouring and hunting ability. Before the 17th century, Spaniels were all considered to be part of the same breed group, but over the years they were separated according to their traits.

The English Cocker Spaniel became part of the small land Spaniel group, separated from the Springer Spaniel, which was a different size. In 1892 the Cocker was registered by the UK Kennel Club.

Character

Cocker Spaniels have a great temperament, and are generally quite happy-go-lucky dogs. They make an excellent family pet because of their small size and their ability to tolerate children. They usually behave well around strangers and are relatively easy to train. They are very sociable and adore the company of others, making them a great first time pet.

They can be so sweet natured and gentle that sometimes they can become quite reserved if they aren't properly socialised. However, the opposite can also happen and they can become quite clingy, focusing on one member of the family, if they aren't taught to be independent. As always, the best way to a happy dog is through proper socialisation, which is discussed here in later chapters.

Health

Cocker Spaniels are happy, laid back dogs but they do suffer from certain health conditions from time to time. Ailments that they are particularly prone to include: skin and ear allergies, cataracts, cancer, deafness, Progressive Retinal Atrophy (PRA), Canine Hip Dysplasia

(CHD), patellar luxation, kidney disease, and cardiomyopathy. Cocker Spaniels also have a high risk of developing eye problems, and blindness can set in as early as 10 years of age.

It should be noted that deafness is a major health concern in parti-coloured Cockers while CHD is prevalent in solid coloured Cockers. All in all, they have a medium level susceptibility to illness when compared to other breeds. They have a lifespan of about 12-15 years, and usually give birth to about 6 puppies in each litter.

Height:
Bitch - Min 36cm (14") / Max 41cm (16")
Dog - Min 38cm (15") /Max 43cm (17")

Weight:
Bitch - Min 12kg (26 lbs)/ Max 15 kg (32 lbs)
Dog - Min 13kg (28 lbs) / Max 16 kg (34 lbs)

Grooming

Cockers need professional grooming 3-4 times a year, thus grooming costs must be carefully considered. Apart from professional grooming, they will need grooming at home once a week, in order to keep their short-medium length coat in tip top condition. The good news is that they tend to shed very little. Spaniel's ears tend to hang low, and so you might need to trim the fur on the ears now and then to keep them from getting dirty and matted.

Exercise

All dogs need plenty of exercise to stay happy and healthy, and the Cocker Spaniel is no exception. You should give your Cocker exercise in the region of 40-60 minutes per day. Remember that he was originally meant to be a gun dog, so he will really enjoy sniffing scents and retrieving. In fact, he will make a fantastic companion on walks.

Cocker Spaniel Facts

Here are some amazing facts about the English Cocker Spaniel:

English Cocker Spaniels are well known for wagging their tails even when hunting.

The English Cocker Spaniel is a distinct breed from the American Cocker Spaniel. However, before the 1930's, they were viewed as belonging to the same breed.

In 2004, the English Cocker Spaniel gained 3rd place in AKC's top ten popular breeds of dogs.

One of the most popular English Cocker Spaniels was named "Shannon", owned by John Kennedy.

The breed got its nickname "Cocker" from being an excellent woodcock hunter.

English Cocker Spaniels are among the most popular therapy dogs because of their affectionate nature and loving dispositions.

Aside from flushing out game birds from the thick underbrush, they are also known to have natural retrieving instincts.

Cockers came from England but trace their ancestors to Spaniels in Spain.

The Cocker's long floppy ears make it prone to ear infections.

Puppy Guide

Preparing for your Cocker Spaniel Puppy

The arrival of a Cocker Spanielpuppy is bound to be a exciting time for any family. In order to avoid last-minute problems with the puppy's needs, it is good to prepare beforehand to ensure the puppy's comfort and your peace of mind.

Here are some of the important things that you should include in your list:

- Crate
- Puppy pen
- Puppy chew toys
- Collar with identification tags and a bell

- Towels or blankets
- Puppy litter box and shavings
- Food and water bowls
- Grooming supplies
- Odour neutraliser

Puppy proofing your home

- Keep any electrical cords out of sight by taping them to the back of cabinets or on walls. Make sure that they cannot be easily reached by your puppy.
- Dangerous chemicals such as insecticides, detergents, disinfectants, and antiseptics should be kept in cupboards with locks or on high shelves.
- Plants should be taken outside the house
- Move breakable things to cabinets which are out of reach
- Gates and crates should be installed
- Rubbish and recycling containers are placed in areas which are inaccessible to your puppy .
- The bathroom door should always be kept closed and the toilet seat should always be down
- An enclosure which is escape-proof should be installed in your garden
- Block the staircases with baby gates

Meeting the Breeder

If you are thinking of bringing home a Cocker Spanielpuppy, you should be certain that you are dealing with a dog breeder who has an excellent reputation in the industry. When you setting up an appointment with a dog breeder, arm yourself with a list of questions that will help you decide.

Knowing whether or not you are dealing with a reputable breeder can help you avoid fly-by-night dog breeders who are into the business for the money without any consideration for the quality and soundness of their litter. Most of their puppies have higher risks of developing inherited health problems that will be surely be just a waste of your money.

Are the puppy's parents certified by a registered vet?
A responsible dog breeder takes the time to have his dogs evaluated
for congenital problems and certified by a vet before mating.

Can you visit the kennel and meet the puppies and their parents?
A dog breeder with a good reputation has nothing to hide and will
gladly welcome you and take you on a tour of the kennel. When
you meet the parents and the litter, be sure to keep a keen eye on the
temperament of the parents and how big they are so you will have an
idea of what your puppy will look like and how it will behave when
full-grown.

How is socialisation conducted while puppies are still in the kennel?
Experts in dog behaviour recommend that socialisation of puppies
should start as early as possible. This is very important because it has
been shown that puppies which are exposed to socialisation between
the ages of 6 and16 weeks old are able to better adjust to new situations, other dogs, and even different people.

Can you see the puppy's vaccination and health record?
When examining the puppy's vaccination and health record, ask
which vaccines the puppy still needs and the schedule of booster
shots. Make sure that the record has been signed by a licensed vet.

Have the puppies been de-wormed?
Puppies already harbour worms when they are born. The mother can
transmit parasites via the placenta when the puppies are still inside
her womb thereby infecting them even before they are whelped. Following a de-worming schedule is very important particularly for very
young puppies which can easily succumb to the effects of parasitism.

Does the breeder provide a guarantee for the sale?
A reputable dog breeder will not hesitate to provide a guarantee for
the purchase of a puppy. This is an important document that will take
care of problems when a puppy that you have bought is later diagnosed with a serious disease condition.

10

Reputable dog breeders provide a certificate of sale, a document that you can use in case problems may crop up later.

Do the parents have pedigree records?
A pedigree record will show you important information on the lineage of the litter for several generations. You will also find records of titles. If you see titles which are listed within the first two generations, these will indicate signs of reliability and soundness of the litter.

Are the puppies fitted with a microchip?
A microchip is one of the best ways of providing dog identity. Although this is very important, not all dog breeders deem it necessary to have their litter micro-chipped.

Can the breeder provide some names of people who have previously brought home puppies from the kennel?
A reputable dog breeder won't hesitate to give you names of people who have bought puppies from his kennel. Once you have the names, take time to call them and ask about their pups and if there were any problems they have encountered.

Advice for Breeders

Introduction to Breeding
It is highly advised that you consult a vet prior to considering breeding a bitch. All the information provided here is researched but it cannot be substituted for sound veterinary care and advice. Breeding is a major responsibility, and must be taken seriously. Before becoming a breeder, you should take advice from the breeder where you acquired your female dog . Don't be under the illusion that breeding is an easy, money-making venture. It will take over all your time, an awful lot of your money and is a lot of hardwork.

Do you have the room?
Before you consider becoming a breeder, make sure you have the room. Puppies are small and cute but they require a lot of space and leave the place messy. As a rule of thumb, you will need large runs

enough to house 10-12 puppies, and whelping boxes. You will also need to wash the bedding once or twice a day, and have a secure outside area.

Can you provide constant care?

A responsible breeder is always ready to provide care to the sire and dam. As a matter of fact, good puppies are possible only if the parents are looked after long before the puppies are born. Make sure you will be able to provide:

- Screening for genetic problems
- Veterinary care
- Good nutrition
- Regular exercise
- Pre-breeding health tests

Also make sure the parent dogs do not feel stressed and maintain a healthy mental state.

Do you have the time?

Make sure you will have sufficient time to attend the dam in the days leading to her labour. You will even need to give a hand for the whelping which typically takes 24 hours. The female Cocker Spaniel should be ready to breed 12 days after her first coloured discharge. Will you have time to make arrangements with the stud and board your female Cocker Spaniel there for a few days?

Will you be able to do frequent check-ups?

The female must be in good health before breeding. Make sure she is not too fat or too thin. Any health issue, even the slightest one, in the mother could be passed on to the new born pups. It is absolutely essential that you take her to the vet frequently and do check-ups to make sure she does not possess any health issues, mental or physical. For example, the female should be fully wormed. Any skin conditions should be addressed, too.

Do you know your legal responsibilities?

According to the Breeding and Sale of Dogs Act 1999, if someone embarks on a career of breeding dogs, they must get a license should the female dog give birth to 5 or more litters in any given period of

12 months.

The breeder must adhere to the following:

Preparing the bitch
The minimum age for breeding Cocker Spanielbitches is 12 months. The breeder must make sure the female is mature enough to give birth to litters. During these 12 months, the breeder must provide the bitch with good nutrition, training and health care and make sure they are going to be a healthy mother of puppies. It is impossible for us to include here all the necessary information a breeder needs to know how to prepare the bitch for breeding, so please contact your vet.

How to choose a stud?
It is very important that you, as a breeder, choose the right sire for your litters. Take professional advice from an experienced breeder and find the perfect stud.

Litter and Puppy Registration

As a breeder, you should register your litter with the Kernel Club. Complete the application to deliver the correct paperwork to the buyers of your pups. Once the registration is completed, you will be sent a registration form by the Kennel Club for you to give to the buyers of your pups so they too can register with the Kernel Club.

More info available on: http://www. thekennelclub.org.uk

13

Protecting your
Cocker Spaniel from Parasites

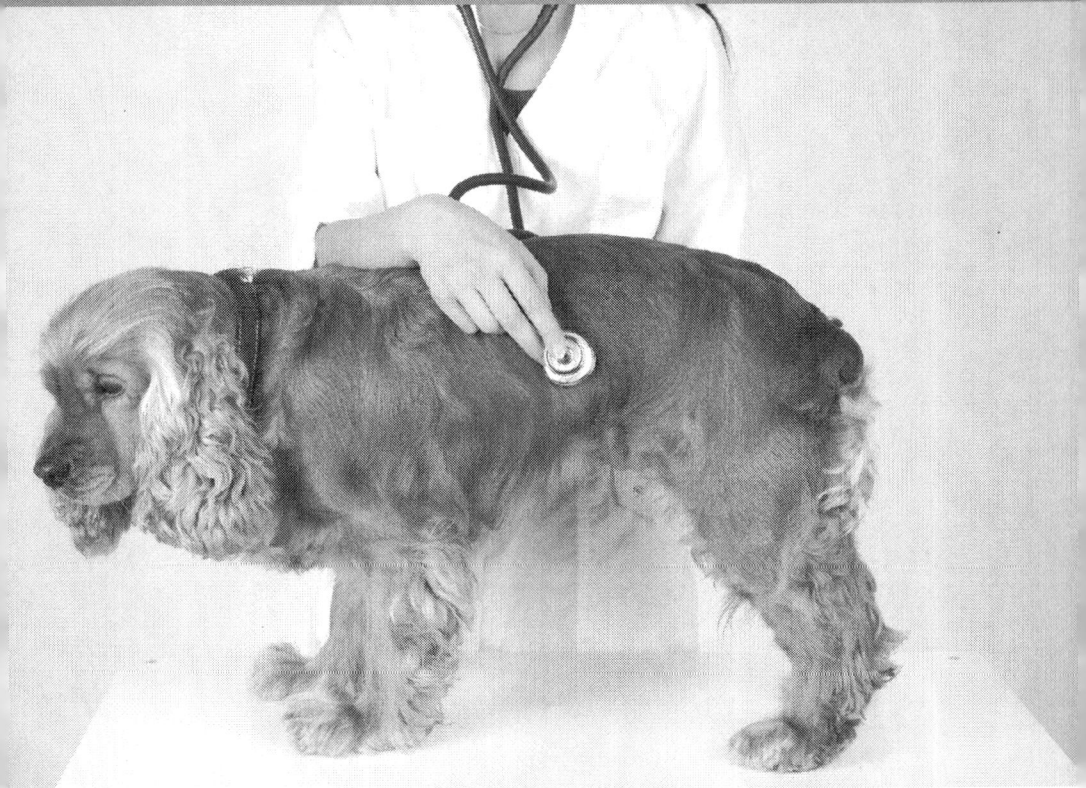

Cocker Spaniels can be affected by fleas and worms at all stages of their lives. Puppies are likely to be infected with worms even before birth! The good news is that there are plenty of things you can do to deal with the problem.

Fleas

Fleas are nasty little parasites. An infestation can be unpleasant and possibly even dangerous for your pet, yourself and your family.

Fleas feed on your pet's blood and in serious cases they can make your pet anaemic. This can cause your dog to become extremely unwell, possibly even critically ill. Fleas cause severe itching, which may lead to fur loss and sores from continual scratching. Their bites are equally uncomfortable for humans, causing intense itching, redness and inflammation.

To be able to treat fleas effectively, it is good idea to understand how their life cycle works. This comprises three stages:

Stage 1
The adult flea jumps onto your pet and begins feeding on their blood. This is when irritation begins and your dog begins scratching.

Stage 2
Within 48 hours, the fleas will begin to lay their eggs, which will fall off your pet into their surroundings (i.e. your home). A female flea can lay up to 50 eggs per day and 10 females can lay up to 15,000 eggs!

Stage 3
Within days all these eggs will hatch into flea larvae. Because the larvae don't like light they crawl into dark areas (such as carpets, cracks and crevices) around your home. The larvae then turn into adult fleas and Stage 1 begins anew…

Statistics show that only 5% of fleas in your home will actually be living on your dog – the other 95% (eggs and larvae) will actually be living in your carpets and furniture. It's therefore essential that the problem is dealt with before it gets out of control.

When your dog has fleas, you may see black specks throughout their coat (these are flea droppings – to be sure, drop these grits in water and it will become a rust colour, this indicates they are definitely from fleas and this rust colour is actually blood) or they may be scratching more than normal, possibly to the extent that they start losing fur.

You should immediately seek advice from your vet on what flea products are right for your dog and the environment they live in to prevent the problem escalating. There are many flea products available, but please be aware some only kill the adult fleas on your pet at the time of using the treatment and won't kill adults around the home, which will be able to just jump back on.

Worms

Worms are an internal parasite that will affect your dog throughout their entire life if left unchecked. Worms can cause many undesirable side effects to your pet's health such as diarrhoea, vomiting, a swollen abdomen, discomfort and respiratory problems. In some cases, worms carried by our pets can cause some very serious side-effects in adults and children. Fortunately, regular treatment can prevent this.

Some common types of worms are:

Roundworms

Roundworms are the most common internal parasite in dogs. Puppies are likely to be infected at birth, because roundworm larvae can be directly passed onto the young via their mother's milk. Other ways your dog may become infected with roundworms are from eating a mouse or rat that may have eaten roundworm eggs.

The roundworm can also be passed between animals by contact with infected faeces. Roundworm infections can be passed to humans and if left untreated can cause serious health problems (including blindness). If children play in areas such as sand or dirt piles that contain infected faeces they may pick up worm larvae on their hands. If their hands aren't washed properly, the child could ingest the larvae when eating or sucking their thumb and end up with roundworms.

Tapeworms

Your dog may become infected with tapeworm when they groom themselves. This is because they may eat fleas or lice in their coats which have previously fed on a tapeworm. They can also become infected by eating infected rodents.

The tapeworm lives in the small intestine and steals lots of the nutrients from the food your dog eats. You may even see parts of the tapeworm, which looks like a rice grain, under your dogs's tail, or in their faeces. The best treatment for tapeworm is to make sure your dog is free from fleas and regularly de-wormed.

Hookworms

Hookworms are most commonly found in dogs, puppies and kittens. Your pet becomes infected with them when the hookworm larvae penetrate the skin or lining of the mouth, or when infected faeces are eaten. They can also be passed on to puppies via the mother's milk.

Hookworms are dangerous – they actually bury into the intestines and suck the blood. If untreated they can have life threatening affects, such as blood loss, weakness and malnutrition. Just like roundworms, hookworm larvae can also be accidentally passed onto humans and cause severe problems when the larvae enter the skin or intestines.

It is always best to prevent worms rather than simply treating the problem once your pet is already suffering from their effects. So, contact your vet early on to plan the best worm treatment for your dog. Pregnant or young animals will require different treatments to adult pets, so your vet's advice is essential.

The Importance of Vaccination

It's really important to make sure that your dog is protected by vaccination from the most common diseases. Vaccines have considerably reduced the number of pets that die from fatal diseases each year, so there's simply no reason not to make sure your dog is fully protected. Bear in mind that any cat or dog travelling abroad requires a rabies vaccination by law.

Your dog

Most puppies will inherit a temporary immunity to nasty diseases from their mother, but this only lasts until around 8 weeks old, so it is advisable to begin the puppy vaccination course at this point. This involves two vaccines administered 2 weeks apart, which helps to obtain good adult immunity. We then recommend that your dog has a yearly booster vaccination.

The Truth about Neutering

The decision to neuter your dog is never easy – something not helped by the many 'old wives tales' on this subject (none of which are actually supported by medical research). It goes without saying that neutering prevents unwanted pregnancies, but it actually has benefits beyond that.

For any pet, neutering presents both advantages and disadvantages, so do some research before making your decision.

Should I have my dog neutered?

Bitches

Despite what many people claim, there is no evidence that allowing a bitch to have a litter of puppies will enhance their character in any way. Pregnancy isn't easy for the bitch and complications can occur at any time – especially during labour. Sometimes an emergency caesarean is required, which can be risky for both the bitch and the puppies.

An un-neutered female comes into season approximately every 6 months. She will become receptive to un-neutered males and could escape to try and find a mate. This often leads to other problems such as fighting, traffic accidents, or even getting lost.

Un-neutered bitches can suffer from a condition called 'false pregnancy or phantom pregnancy' which may require veterinary treatment. This is permanently eliminated when they are neutered.

There is evidence to show if a bitch is neutered before reaching maturity she is less likely to develop breast tumours in later life.

A life-threatening illness called pyometra (an infection of the uterus) is also prevented by neutering. This disease can present complications even after surgery if the infection has leaked from the uterus and can lead to peritonitis, but neutering prevents it altogether.

Neutering your bitch does present two disadvantages, but they are negligible when compared to the benefits.

- Due to hormonal changes, your bitch may be more prone to weight gain after neutering. However, this can easily be prevented through proper diet and regular exercise.
- In a very small percentage of bitches (normally pure breed setters, spaniels etc.) there can be a slight alteration in their coat's texture

and colour.

The most up-to-date research recommends neutering the bitch before her first season, ideally when they are around 6-8 months old. After this, a season may be about to start, when neutering would then need to be delayed, because of the higher risk of bleeding if the operation was carried out at that time.

If your dog has had a season she can still be neutered, but would have to wait 2-3 months after the season has finished..

Males
Neutering will remove the sexual urge in male dogs s, if your dog got the scent of a bitch in season, he would be unlikely to show any interest in her. In the case of an un-neutered dog, he would show great interest and the same unwanted effects as with the bitch can occur with the male, e.g. road traffic accidents, fighting and straying far from home. You will be able to keep male and female dogs living together happily all year round.

There is no evidence that castrated males have any dramatic changes to their original temperament. However, neutered males will generally be much easier to train,and less likely to want to dominate due to the reduction of testosterone in their system and, therefore, less likely to be distracted as they would no longer be constantly looking for a mate.

When the male dog is neutered their testicles are removed, so they will not develop testicular cancer – which is common in un-castrated male dogs as they get older.

A neutered male dog is also less likely to suffer from prostate problems and cancers associated with their anus.

The male dog is best neutered between 6-8 months, this will stop scent-marking indoors and other unwanted behaviour becoming a habit.

Learn to Spot Early Warning Signs

You know your Cocker Spaniel best and if you notice any abnormal symptoms or changes in behaviour, do not hesitate to visit your vet for advice or reassurance. Vets love to talk with you about your animals, and will always be pleased to give their professional advice!

Even if it turns out to be something completely innocuous, you'll still have the peace of mind that comes from knowing they're in good health.

Some signs to look out for include:
- Change in weight (loss or gain)
- Changes in appetite
- Increased thirst
- Lethargy
- Stiffness/reluctance to exercise as normal
- Change in their coat
- Changes in urination patterns (including incontinence)
- Coughing and wheezing
- Breathlessnessx
- Vomiting, diarrhoea or constipation
- Smelly breath
- Eyesight or hearing problems
- Lumps or bumps

It is important to make sure your dog has twice-yearly check-ups with their vet. This will help to make sure any illnesses or health problems they may be suffering from are detected in the earliest stages.

Keeping Your Golden Retriever's Teeth Healthy

Dental disease is the number one health disorder found in dogs over 3 years of age, with more than 80% of dogs suffering from some form of dental disease.

Dental disease has been referred to as a 'silent killer' of our pets -the bacteria on your pet's teeth can move into the blood stream where it is free to travel to the heart, liver, lungs and kidneys. This will have a serious effect on your dog's overall health and may even compromise their immune system. Maintaining the health of your dog's teeth is therefore one of the most important things you can do to increase the comfort and length of their life.

People often mistakenly think that because their dog is eating, their teeth are fine. However, this is not necessarily the case. A dog's survival instinct is very strong, so it will continue to eat even with extremely sore and rotten teeth.

Our dogs usually start life with shiny white teeth and healthy pink gums. Over time, the accumulation of plaque (bacteria) on the surface of the teeth will lead to inflammation of the gums (gingivitis). This will then lead to an accumulation of tartar (bacteria and minerals) on the surface of the teeth (and very bad breath!). If left untreated, bacteria will penetrate below the gum-line and can destroy supportive structures (periodontitis), leading to tooth-loss and abscesses.

Just think of any bad experiences you've had with toothache. Untreated dental conditions are just as painful for pets as for people, so it's essential they are dealt with -and even better if they are prevented from occurring in the first place. The good news is that dental disease is preventable if treated early enough, so have your vet regularly check your dog's teeth for any early warning signs.

Treatment at the vet involves a light anaesthetic and possible dental x-rays. These will give the vet a clear picture of the health of the tooth roots and the jaw, as these crucial areas are not visible to the naked eye. The vet will clean all the teeth with an ultrasonic dental machine, which cleans away the bacteria beneath the gum line. Afterwards, the vet will assess each tooth individually and decide if further treatment is required. If the dental disease has progressed too far on some of the teeth, the vet will recommend a tooth extraction. It may sound drastic, but it will solve the problem once and for all and leave your pet much more comfortable in the future.

There's also plenty you can do at home to take care of your dog's teeth. It is best to start dental home care when your pet is young. This is one of the most important things to help prevent dental disease. Introduce regular tooth brushing while your dog is still young, so they become used to it. This will help to prevent the build-up of plaque. However, some dental diseases are genetic, so home care can cure the symptoms, but never get rid of the disease completely. A wide range of home care products are available, including chews, toys and mouth washes. However, it has been proven that brushing is the number one preventative measure owners can take. As always, ask your vet if you need advice about which products are right for your dog.

Food and Diet

Some Cocker Spaniels can be fussy eaters, so you must discourage any fussiness by introducing various foods and remove the bowl after 20 minutes if they are messing about with it and not eating. They will soon learn to eat their meal in the first sitting, so to speak, and be keen to eat whatever you put down for them.

To stop your dog becoming possessive over its food bowl, add tasty morsels while they are eating, so they get used to your hand and fingers being in their bowl. Your vet and/or breeder can give you advice on the best diet for your dog. Don't allow your dog to become overweight as this will take you straight to your vet with the various health problems that are present in an overweight dog.

Creating a balanced diet

Your choice of food is probably the most important influence that you can have on your dog's health. If your pet is to live a long and healthy life, it's essential that you give them the right food. There are so many diets available on the market with a huge variation in cost and quality. This can be confusing when you are trying to decide what to feed your dog.

With pet food, you really do get what you pay for, so do get advice from your vet on the best quality food to suit your dog's individual dietary requirements. Be prepared to pay a little extra if necessary, as the difference to your dog's health will more than justify the cost.

Quality foods will cost a little more, due to their high nutritional value and low water content, but this is offset by the fact that your dog will eat less and feel fuller. Bags of top quality food will also last for longer, so the overall cost can work out as being similar to the cheaper bags in the long run.

Alternatively, you could feed your dog a home-prepared diet. There are currently two major schools of thought in veterinary medicine; the majority of practitioners favour manufactured foods, whereas a small, but a growing, minority advocate home-prepared diets. Both sides are equally convinced that their method is best.

If you decide to take this route, get your vet's advice and do lots of research in advance. A balanced diet contains a variety of ingredients to supply the body with all the nutrients it needs. A poor diet will almost certainly lead to health problems, so make sure your dog is getting all the nutrition they need.

Why you should cut down on treats

There can be a number of reasons why your Cocker Spaniel might become overweight. However, the most likely cause is an unsuitable diet and a lack of sufficient exercise.

Food plays an important role on your dog's overall health and well-being. A nutritious, balanced and healthy diet is an essential part of an active lifestyle, and a big part of that is resisting the temptation to give them human food as treats.

Although it may seem harmless, if your dog begins to expect occasional treats like this, it can have a serious effect on their overall health.

As you can see, these foods can be extremely unhealthy for your pets, even in small amounts. It's therefore essential that you resist the temptation to offer treats like this (no matter how much they beg!). There are plenty of healthy dog treats available which dogs love, so keep a supply of those around the house instead.

Signs that your Cocker Spaniel is overweight include the following:
- You can't easily feel the ribs when running your hands along your their sides
- There is no obvious slimming at your dog's waist
- Their collar or harness may become tight and need loosening
- They may not exercise as much as usual and become tired quickly
- Slow, lethargic movement
- Shortness of breath
- Stiffness in joints
- Sleeping more than normal
- Bad temper
- Unable to groom certain areas of their body (normally around the lower spine). As a result, their fur may become matted and scruffy-looking.

If you feel your dog is showing any of the signs above contact your vet. They will be able to offer advice on weight loss and healthy eating for your pet.

When planning a diet for your dog, pick a high-quality food that's rich in protein. There are many foods available but, some will be more suited to your dog than others, so don't be afraid to ask your vet for advice if you're unsure.

Common Diseases in Dogs

Brimming with energy, it's all too easy to imagine that dogs get by without a health-care in the world. However, just like any other species – not least humans – there are all manner of ailments that can happen to canines. From viral and bacterial infections picked up in the big wide world to rare congenital disorders and cancer.

What's more, just like us, dogs can all too easily fall prey to lifestyle-related health troubles. We're well aware of the effects of a sedentary lifestyle and a poor diet on our own health; such factors impact on dogs in very much the same way, with diabetes and heart disease the common results. Finally, just as with humans, canine old age brings its own set of health issues, from arthritis to failing eyesight.

Fortunately, if dogs have much in common with people in the diversity of health problems they can potentially face, they also benefit from vast advances in medical knowledge and care. We now know far more about the diseases that trouble dogs than we once did, and with a little knowledge dog-owners can spot early warning signs, and also take measures to help ward off the threat of many diseases. Here are some common dog diseases you should familiarise yourself with.

Addison's disease in dogs

Addison's disease is known in medical terms as "hypoadrenocorticism". It happens when the outer area of a dog's adrenal glands stop producing enough hormones. Here are some important things to know about Addison's disease and how to spot it in your dog.

How does Addison's disease affect the adrenal glands?

Your dog has two adrenal glands, one beside each kidney. These glands produce special substances which regulate a number of important bodily functions. Two of these substances are hormones called cortisol and aldosterone, and when these are deficient in the body it results in a conditions called Addison's disease.

What causes Addison's?

One of the most common causes is an injury to the adrenal gland. This might be because of an infection, haemorrhage, or an immune system condition.

Other causes include:
- Sudden withdrawal from cortisone, a steroid treatment
- Treatment for Cushings (the opposite of Addison;s, where too much cortisol is produced)
- Dysfunction of the pituitary gland in the brain

What are the symptoms of Addison's disease in dogs?

The symptoms of Addison's are not specifically associated with Addison's, and might also be linked to problems like tummy upsets or kidney diseases. So, it's important not to jump to conclusions before seeing a vet.

The main symptoms to look out for include:
- Vomiting
- Weight loss
- Diarrhoea
- Thirst
- Increased urination
- Episodes of shaking or trembling

When is it serious?

An "Addisonian crisis" can happen in acute cases. This might involve collapse, sudden weakness, vomiting, and diarrhoea. When these symptoms appear out of nowhere, it's important to get urgent medical attention for your dog.

Lots of laboratory blood tests will need to be carried out to get an accurate diagnosis. Your dog may well be taken into vet care overnight as a result.

How is Addison's disease treated?

It's important to be aware that your dog might need treatment for life, as the hormones involved are so vital to their well-being. Regular visits to the vet will be needed to make sure the treatment is working at the correct dose, and at certain periods it will need to be increased or decreased, for example in period at times of illness or stress.

Once Addison's has been diagnosed though, it can usually be managed fairly successfully with the use of oral tablets. There's no need to alter your dog's activity or diet. At first, the dog's progress will need to be monitored carefully to avoid complications, and this could involve an overnight stay or two at the vet's. Once things have stabilised though, there's an excellent chance that your dog will live a long and happy life with the right care and attention.

Aural haematoma (blood blisters in the ears)

Haematoma sounds complicated but is actually an area of clotted blood which can occur anywhere in your dog's body. It looks like a bruise or a blood blister and the most common place you'll find it is in the flap of the ears. Here, we'll look at the ears in particular and what might be causing the haematoma.

Why do these haematomas appear in my dog's ear?

Infections and irritations of the ear happen a lot with dogs, especially in breeds with dropped ears like Spaniels and Bassets. When the ear canal is itchy, dogs will scratch the area vigorously and sometimes shake their heads repeatedly. This causes damage to the delicate blood vessels in the ear flaps. The result is bleeding and the appearance of blood blisters. These blisters can sometimes spread to the whole ear area, causing further irritation and worsening the problem.

How can these blisters be treated?

It's important that the vet diagnoses the root cause of the haematoma, before proceeding with treatment. Most times, the culprit will be an infection of the ear canal, which is the cause of all the scratching and shaking. The swelling that happens because of this needs to be treated. The fluid in the ear will need to be drained and this can be done using either a syringe or with surgery. If surgery is required, the ear flap will have stitches scattered across it to keep the pouch closed to allow the natural process of healing.

Does the blister ever disappear by itself?

A blood blister is just like a bruise, and because of this it's theoretically possible for it to heal by itself. However, with all the irritation and scratching it usually causes, the blister is more likely to increase in size and cause even more discomfort if it's left untreated. In a worse case scenario, the clots are left to form a fibrous tissue that distorts the ear, a condition called "cauliflower ear" that's often irreversible.

If you've spotted a blood blister that's causing your dog lots of irritation, the best thing to do is to take your dog to the vet and get things addressed early on. As with all dog ailments, early treatment is the best way to a happy pet!

Babesiosis: a tick borne disease

Babesiosis is a tick borne disease that is spread when a tick infected with a certain parasite (Babesia canis) bites your dog. The infection causes a destruction of the red blood cells, resulting in your dog becoming anaemic and jaundiced. Here, we'll explain how this tick borne disease occurs and what you can do about it.

What are the symptoms of Babesiosis?

Babesiosis mainly affects younger dogs and puppies who have no built in immunity to the illness. It can't be passed from one dog to another, and is only spread by ticks. It is relatively new in the UK and has become a problem since quarantine laws were relaxed and pets began to travel more frequently throughout Europe.

Some of the signs and symptoms of the disease include:
- Depression
- Weakness
- Loss of appetite
- Pale gums, lips, tongue or eyelids
- Fever
- Dark coloured urine

How does the disease spread?

It's caused by various types of single celled organisms, and is found in both domestic and wild animals. These parasites can't survive outside of the dog or the tick host, and it takes up to three days for the dog to become infected once the tick has started feeding on it. Luckily, it can't be caught by humans. Until recently, the disease has only been a problem with dogs in quarantine, but since the introduction of the Pet Passport Scheme there have been several cases reported in Britain.

I want to take my dog abroad. Is there a danger they will catch Babesiosis?

That depends on whether you're visiting an affected area. The ticks are known to be prevalent in Southern Europe especially. Under the Pet Passport Scheme, pets are required to be treated for ticks before they return to Britain to avoid these diseases spreading.

How will I know if my dog has been infected during this time?

If your dog has been infected while you were away, they may not show any symptoms for 10-20 days. Signs of the disease can be mild, from being a bit "off colour" to serious, with a lack of appetite, dark urine, and in severe cases organ failure and death.

It's important to note that in mild cases, the dog might recover completely but may still be a carrier for the parasite, and could spread it to ticks that are native to Britain. So, treatment is important regardless of how serious the symptoms are.

How is Babesiosis treated?

The good news is, there are drugs available which will treat the disease quite effectively, provided a diagnosis has been made in time. If your dog is showing any of the symptoms mentioned in this article, it's important to get them to a vet as soon as possible. Be sure to tell your vet that your dog has been to a different country, as this will help with diagnosis.

How can I prevent my dog becoming infected while we're away?

You should practice a thorough tick control routine while you're away. This should include spraying the dog with an anti-tick treatment, grooming them regularly and removing any ticks that you find on a daily basis. You should also pay special attention to their sleeping area and spray that too. Special anti-tick collars are available if your dog has a real problem with sprays but these aren't as effective, so you'll need to pay extra attention to removing ticks.

Bladder stones (Cystic Calculi)

Bladder stones or "cystic calculi" as they are known in medical terms, can develop in lots of areas of the body including the gall bladder and kidneys. Here, we'll explain some of the problems that bladder stones can cause in dogs, and what can be done about them.

How do bladder stones affect a dog?

The symptoms of bladder stones are very similar to those of cystitis. They include:
- Blood stained urine: Haematuria or bloody urine occurs when the stones irritate the delicate lining of the bladder, causing inflammation and bleeding. Sometimes a bacterial infection will make the problem worse.

- Straining to urinate: The inflammation of the bladder wall causes a lot of irritation, and creates the urge to urinate even when the dog doesn't need to go.
- Painful abdomen: When the tube which carries the urine from the bladder is blocked it can cause a lot of pain. Touching the dog's abdomen might make them yelp with discomfort.

How do bladder stones happen?

A particular compound in the urine, when present in large amounts, causes the stones to form. This can happen as a result of something in the dog's diet, or because of a bladder infection. Very rarely, the stones are caused by a fault in the dog's body chemistry which is found in certain breeds.

How long does it take for the stones to form?

This depends on lots of factors, including how bad the bladder infection (cystitis) is, and how much of the crystal forming compound is present in the urine, as well as how acidic the urine is. Larger bladder stones can take months or years to grow, and can go undetected for a long time. Some stones have been known to develop very quickly and cause blockages in a matter of weeks.

How will my vet diagnose bladder stones?

The presence of bladder stones can usually be detected by:
- Analysing the urine
- Feeling the abdomen for larger stones
- Looking for the stones with an X-ray
- Ultrasounds can be used if x-rays aren't conclusive

How are bladder stones treated?

There are a few ways bladder stones can be treated, depending on how serious they are and if they are causing a major blockage (which is usually seen as an emergency).

These include:
- Surgery to remove the stones
- Antibiotics to treat the infection
- Drugs to treat the acidity of the urine
- Special diets to dissolve the stones and prevent them from coming back

In most cases, the prognosis is good for dogs who are treated for bladder stones. The main thing is to prevent them coming back again by keeping a close eye on your dog's behaviour and diet.

Breast cancer in dogs

Breast cancer is a very common form of cancer in female dogs, second only to skin cancer. It can happen in both benign (not harmful) and malignant (harmful) forms. Don't panic if you find a lump in your dog's breast; 60% of these lumps are found to be benign and won't cause any complications. Here, we'll explain some of the more frequently asked questions about breast cancer and how it's treated.

Which dogs are prone to getting breast cancer?

Breast cancer usually occurs in female dogs, mostly those aged eight or over. Purebred dogs are more likely to get breast cancer than mongrels, with the breeds most at risk being Spaniels, Poodles and Terriers. Other susceptible breeds include Beagles, Greyhounds and Cocker Spaniels but these breeds tend to have a lower risk of the tumour being malignant.

How is the cancer detected?

You may have noticed a swelling of one of the breasts while grooming your dog. These swellings can either be firm nodules that move when touched, or soft lumps that are stuck to the tissues underneath. Or, there might be a few small nodules that are only a few millimeters in diameter.

It's thought that 70% of the tumours are found in those mammary glands towards the tail end. Sometimes, the affected teat will secrete fluid. In very serious cases, the tumours may have spread to other organs such as the lungs, causing shortness of breath. If you spot any of these lumps or bumps you should contact your vet as soon as possible to get them checked out.

What causes breast cancer in dogs?

We don't know the exact cause of these cancers, but we do know that they are related to hormones.

How are the tumours treated?

This depends on how far the tumour has progressed. Your dog might need to have a mastectomy to remove the breast completely, just as people with breast cancer do. Or, there might be a lumpectomy, where just the lump itself is removed. You might find that the wound is quite big after surgery. Don't be alarmed if this happens - it's important to remove as large an area as possible to ensure all the tumour cells are removed and this will help to stop the tumour growing back.

It's important to note that some dogs might be considered too old and frail to have major surgery. So, their tumours will be monitored closely instead, and a biopsy will be taken to investigate further.

Later on, if a lump is found to be malignant (harmful) then your dog might need to have chemotherapy, but the majority of lumps (60%) are benign.

Is there any way to prevent my dog getting breast cancer?

The best way of preventing this cancer is to get your dog neutered when it's young, ideally before her first season and definitely before her second or third.

Cataracts

A cataract is when the lens of a dog's eye becomes opaque or cloudy instead of being clear. It can cause problems with a dog's eyesight. Here is some useful information about cataracts and what can be done about them.

What causes cataracts?

Some of the most common causes of cataracts include:
- Diabetes
- Old age
- Genetic inheritance

There are certain breeds of dog that are prone to getting cataracts and these include American Cockers, Cocker Spaniel and Cocker Spaniels, Poodles, Boston Terriers and Staffordshire Bull Terriers.

Do cataracts cause blindness?

This depends on how much of the lens is affected by the cataract. Your dog's vision will be affected if the cataract covers about 60% or more of the lens. If the cataract progresses to cover 100% of the lens, a dog will no longer be able to see. Not all cataracts will get progressively worse though – some stay static.

Is there any way to stop my dog from going blind?

If the lens has become really opaque, your vet can refer you to an eye specialist to have it surgically removed. Whilst there's no guarantee this will correct things, there is a good chance that it will restore your dog's vision.

Do only very old dogs go blind?

That really depends on the breed of dog. Some breeds will develop cataracts very early on in life and can lose their sight at a young age. Others will only develop cataracts when they are fairly old. Some cataracts will progress so slowly that dogs will be able to see reasonably well into old age.

There are certain eye disease certification schemes which can tell breeders whether they are producing disease free dogs. These are run by organisations such as the British Veterinary Association, the Kennel Club and the International Sheepdog Society. Ask your vet for more details.

Convulsions, (also known as fits or seizures)

A convulsion is not just one form of reaction. In a dog a convulsion can take many forms, from loss of consciousness to incontinence, you dog may also show signs of mental and behavioural changes or twitching of the muscles in the body. A convulsion can be caused by epilepsy, toxins, trauma and tumours in the brain or spinal cord.

What happens during a convulsion?

Usually there are signs before a convulsion takes on its most obvious form and convulsions tend to take three phases:

Phase 1 - The dog may show unusual signs of discomfort or nervousness, this can last from seconds to hours.
Phase 2 – This is the actual convulsion and can last between a few seconds and about five minutes. The dog can experience any or all of the signs mentioned above and if this stage goes on longer than five or ten minutes then it is considered to be an emergency situation.
Phase 3 – This is the recovery period after the fit, the signs here can include disorientation, blindness, restlessness and general discomfort.

Can my dog die?

This is very rare but could happen if a dog is allowed to convulse for more than a few minutes without intervention, if the convulsions become very serious then this is known as epilepticus, and a vet should be contacted immediately if this situation arises. Please be aware that while this can be frightening to watch, the dog is not thought to be in pain during a convulsion.

What should I do while the seizure is progressing?

- Time the length of each phase so you know how serious the convulsion might be, and can tell your vet if necessary.
- Make sure that the dog is on the ground away from any dangerous items so he can't fall off anything or hurt himself further.
- Turn off any lights and close the curtains as light can affect a convulsion.
- Call your vet if at all concerned.

Can anything be done to prevent further fits?

Drugs can be provided over a period of one to two weeks to prevent fits, if successful the dosage is decreased over a period of time – the time it takes to do this is dependent on the severity of the original convulsions and the dosage provided to the dog. Nevertheless, it is very important that you don't just immediately stop giving your dog the drugs completely as this can make the convulsions worse.

Coronavirus

Coronavirus is a common intestinal infection which tends to hit young puppies. Like other intestinal viruses, it is spread through the faeces of infected dogs, and then picked up by others through contaminated places, or by directed contact with a sick dog. Fortunately, the disease is often quite mild – little more than a passing tummy bug. However, it can hit younger puppies hard. Watch out for diarrhoea that comes on suddenly. Your puppy may have very loose and smelly faeces, often orange in colour, and it will generally look very sorry for itself, lethargic and with little interest in its food. If the symptoms don't clear up quickly it's time to contact a vet.

How is it treated?

Unfortunately, there is no treatment for the virus itself – it simply has to run its course. However, there are potential secondary impacts – severe diarrhoea always carries the risk of severe dehydration, so intravenous fluids are sometimes needed in extreme cases. There's also a risk of secondary infections, so antibiotics may be a good idea. Fortunately, however, with treatment and advice from a vet most dogs usually make a full recovery and are back to their usual, bouncy selves before too long.

Can I prevent my dog from getting it?

There's no vaccination for the virus, and the best way to guard against it is cleanliness, particularly if there are other dogs around.

Cysts

Finding lumps and bumps on your dog's skin can be a bit scary. Don't panic though. Whilst it's true that lumps can sometimes be cancerous, there are many other causes that aren't so serious. Here, we'll discuss some of the more benign lumps, or cysts, that can occur and how they can be treated.

What exactly are cysts?

Cysts are lumps that can be found anywhere on your dog's body. They contain fluid which might have solidified over time. Here are some different types of cysts:

Follicular cysts
These are sometimes called epidermoid cysts and are enlarged hair follicles. They contain dark coloured fluid and are prone to becoming infected. Similar to these cysts are dilated pores and black heads (comedones) which have wide openings on the surface.

True cysts
These cysts are usually found where the ducts in glands are blocked, for example in sweat glands. They have a special secretory lining which may have to be removed to prevent them from recurring.

What causes a cyst?

Certain breeds are more prone to cysts than others, including

Schnauzers, Cocker Spaniels and Yorkshire Terriers. It's also common for young dogs to get cysts on their heads.

Some other known causes of cysts include:
- Blocked pores
- Local injuries
- Damage to the pressure points
- Sun damage
- Use of certain medications such as steroids
- Conditions where the skin stops producing sebum
- Reactions to injections
- Haemorrhage or trauma to the area affected

What do cysts look like?

With follicular and dermoid cysts you might find there is an unpleasant discharge, a substance with the texture of soft cheese called keratin. If the cyst is infected with a yeast or bacteria, the cyst can sometimes smell pretty bad. With sweat gland cysts, there might be hair loss in the area. These nodules are a few millimetres in diameter and are usually a translucent blue or dark colour. There may be more than one cyst, and they are more common around the eyes and ears.

It's important to note that cysts that are filled with blood often appear to be very dark in colour. It can be easy to confuse these with cancers before they are fully investigated. Don't worry, your vet will be able to get to the bottom of things with a full examination.

How will my vet diagnose a cyst?

The best way for your vet to tell whether a lump is a cyst or something more serious is through examining the tissue in a laboratory. To do this the vet will usually have to remove some of the cyst, or sometimes the entire lump.

How common are cysts?

Follicular cysts are common in dogs and so are sweat gland cysts, which occur a lot on the eyelids. Cysts that happen because of trauma or injury are moderately common. Dermoid cysts are rare.

Can they be treated?

In most cases, the vet will remove the lump surgically. Sometimes, in special cases, laser treatment can be used. For small follicular cysts, especially ones that are multiple, there are topical treatments that can be used. Cysts that have appeared because of trauma to the area can disappear themselves over time. A lot of the time, a single cyst itself will disappear completely after surgical removal. If there are multiple cysts, your vet might need to do some more investigation into their cause. If your dog is one of the breeds that is more prone to getting cysts, there is always a chance that more will appear in the future.

What can I do for my dog at home?

The best thing you can do is to try and stop them from scratching, rubbing, licking or biting the cyst as this can increase inflammation and cause even more discomfort. Keep any affected areas as clean as you can to prevent infection, particularly after surgery. Keep an eye out for any swelling or bleeding and report anything like this to the vet immediately.

Are the cysts contagious?

No, the good news is there is no risk of your family or other pets because the cysts aren't infectious.

Cystitis

Cystitis happens when the lining of a dog's bladder becomes inflamed. It's a common condition in male and female dogs. Here, we'll explore some of the causes and treatments for the condition.

What causes cystitis?

Most of the time, cystitis is caused by a bacterial infection in the bladder. This infection can either come from outside of the body, via the urethra (ascending) or it can originate inside the body, for example in the kidneys (descending). Cystitis can also be caused by anything that blocks the normal function of the bladder – this could be bladder stones, tumours or even a neurological problem which affects normal bladder functions.

What are the symptoms of cystitis?

The signs can vary according to the underlying cause of the cystitis, but mostly there will be blood in the urine, and the dog will be straining to pee, with only a little bit of urine coming out.

Is cystitis serious?

Apart from being extremely uncomfortable, cystitis can be a sign of something more serious so it's very important at the first signs of any straining to go to the vet. An obstruction in the bladder is one cause of cystitis that is very serious and needs to be seen to immediately. For male dogs it can be especially painful, as they have a longer more narrow urethra.

How will the vet diagnose cystitis?

The vet will take a urine sample and carry out tests to see what the problem is. If you like, you can bring a sample with you to make things easier, although it's vital to make sure the container you use is scrupulously clean beforehand to avoid distorting the results. The vet will also gently feel the dog's bladder for any abnormalities such as thickening or even bladder stones. If there is any doubt, an x-ray or an ultrasound might be taken to investigate whether there are stones or tumours in the bladder area. Blood tests are also an option,e specially if the dog is showing other symptoms such as a low appetite or fever.

How is it treated?

Most of the time the cystitis is caused by a bacterial infection, which can be easily treated with antibiotics. If the cause is bladder stones, surgery or a special diet might be needed to get rid of them.

Diabetes

Diabetes is as much a problem for dogs as it is for people. In fact, the canine experience of this hormonal disorder mirrors our own remarkably closely. And just as with diabetic people the condition can be successfully managed – though you'll have some work to do to keep your diabetic dog healthy.

What is diabetes?

Dogs generally suffer from insulin-dependent diabetes mellitus, better known in humans as Type 1 Diabetes in people. A diabetic dog, just like a diabetic human, cannot produce enough of the hormone insulin. This substance is a vital element in the clever metabolic system in mammals. Produced by the pancreas, it's what allows the energy-giving glucose from food to pass from the blood into the cells – and without that energy we simply can't function.

What are the symptoms?

The classic signs of diabetes in dogs are a ravenous appetite and a raging thirst; and if your dog seems to need to urinate far more than it used to, that too is a tell-tale sign. What is happening inside its body is that glucose is building up in the blood and failing to get through to the cells.

Desperate to fuel its body the dog eats more, but this only raises the glucose levels higher, and with the cells unable to absorb the glucose, it has only one way out – as urine, taking large amounts of fluid with it and setting your dog gasping for more water as dehydration threatens.

What causes diabetes?

The causes of the insulin deficiency behind this condition are many and varied. Diseases of the pancreas or liver can start the problem, as can hormonal conditions, some drugs and certain infections. Obesity too can trigger diabetes. The condition is commonest in older, unneutered bitches, but it can crop up in any dog.

How will the vet treat diabetes?

A vet will usually diagnose diabetes with blood tests if you turn up at the surgery with a dog showing the classic symptoms. The good news is that the condition can be managed, but the bad news is that, just as with diabetes in people, doing so takes a lot of work. For a start you'll need to regularise your dog's diet and exercise routine, and get used to administering a regular daily dose of insulin. You'll also have to learn to watch out for the hypoglycaemic episodes when the artificially administered insulin levels get out of kilter. But happily, once you get over these challenges your diabetic dog will generally be able to enjoy a largely normal life.

Distemper

Distemper is a very contagious disease that is spread by contact with an infected dog. It's also found in other animal species such as ferrets, skunks and even seals. Here are some common questions and answers on the subject of distemper that you may find useful.

How is distemper spread?

Distemper is a virus that can be transmitted from dog to dog via contact. For example, coughing can spread the disease and the mucus from the nose is also heavily infected.

What are the symptoms of distemper?

The main symptoms include:
- Fever
- Loss of appetite
- Thick yellow discharge from the eyes and nose
- Coughing

- Seizures

Lots of other illnesses can cause these symptoms in dogs, but the symptoms are not usually present all at the same time, as they are with distemper. A blood test will help your vet to know for sure.

What can be done to treat it?

Unfortunately, antibiotics don't work on viral infections, but they are often still needed because the virus can cause secondary bacterial infections to develop. Fluids might be given to your dog through a drip, as well as cough suppressants and drugs to treat seizures. Some new antivirals that are used on people have recently been tried on dogs with some success. You might find that your dog also needs some intensive nursing during this time.

Can dogs make a complete recovery from distemper?

Usually they will make a full recovery, but some dogs are left with recurring seizures or nervous twitches afterwards.

How can I stop my dog from catching distemper?

Luckily there is a vaccine available, which is usually given to puppies as a series of injections. A dog should get follow-up vaccinations about every three years and may be more often in areas where the disease is more common. Because of these vaccines, the disease is now at very low levels in the UK. However, your dog might still be at risk of catching it from wild animals such as ferrets, foxes and seals. Stray dogs can also be carriers of the disease, so try to minimise contact with them.

Dry eye

Dry eye is medically known as Keratoconjunctivitis sicca (KCS). It's a condition that's true to its name: the eye stops producing tears and as a result it has a very dry, sore appearance. Here, we'll go through some of the causes and treatments of dry eye and what it means for your dog.

How is dry eye caused?

Dry eye happens when any problem affecting the tear duct stops it from producing tears. Tears are composed of a watery substance as well as mucoid and fatty parts. They are vital for keeping the eyes moist and free from infection.

A number of different factors can cause dry eye, including:
- Autoimmune problems which destroy the glands that produce tears
- Diseases such as distemper
- Drugs such as certain antibiotics
- Diabetes
- Hypothyroidism

Which dogs are prone to dry eye?

The condition is usually found in middle-aged or older dogs. Any breed, whether pedigree or cross-breeds, can be affected. Sometimes, puppies are born with a defect which stops the tear glands developing normally.

Usually though, the following breeds will be especially prone to dry eye:
- West Highland White Terriers
- American Cocker Spaniels
- Lhasa Apsos
- Yorkshire Terriers

What are the symptoms of dry eye?

Dry eye can be acute (it comes on rapidly) or it can be chronic (it happens gradually over time). If there is a tightly closed, painful look-ing eye, or an ulceration of the cornea, then you should seek urgent medical treatment for your dog as these are signs of acute dry eye. Here are some other signs to look out for:

- Conjunctivitis
- Reddened eyes
- Lacklustre appearance in the clear part of the eye
- Sticky discharge

Dry eyes can easily become infected and when this happens, there is a mucoid discharge. Both eyes will usually be affected although one is often worse than the other.

How will my vet diagnose dry eye?

The vet will look for all the usual clinical signs of dry eye. They might also do a special test called a Schirmer Tear test, which involves placing small strips of a special paper under the eyelids to measure the amount of tears being produced. Don't worry, the test doesn't hurt the dog at all.

How is dry eye treated?

Your dog can be treated with eye drops which will help to lubricate the eye and stimulate the production of more tears. Recently new immune suppressant eye ointments have been brought out which have made a huge improvement to the treatment of dry eye. Sometimes your dog might need antibiotic eye ointments to clear up any infections.

In rare cases, where the usual treatments aren't working, your vet may resort to surgery to clear up the problem. The salivary gland ducts can be redirected so that they discharge into the eye and this is often effective because tears share many of the same properties as saliva. This procedure is very specialised and you will have to be referred to someone with the right expertise (a veterinary ophthalmologist).to carry it out. (

What can I do to prevent my dog from getting dry eye?

There are a few things you can do, including the following:
- Protect your dog from getting the infections that can cause dry

eye, for example by vaccinating them against diseases like distemper
- Avoid any drugs where the side effects are known to cause dry eye
- If your dog has diabetes or hypothyroidism, make sure their tear production is tested regularly

Eyelid problems: ectropion

Ectropion is a problem where the eyelids turn outward. It usually affects the lower lids. Here are a few commonly asked questions about the condition.

What causes ectropion?

One known cause of the condition is hereditary disposition. We know that breeds like Spaniels, Bloodhounds, St Bernards and Newfoundlands are affected more often than other breeds.

Why is ectropion a problem?

The condition causes the delicate lining of the eyelids to be exposed to the air which leads to lots of infections and irritation. When the eyelids droop, the tears tend to spill over and the dog will look like it always has very wet eyes.

How can it be treated?

Surgery is often necessary to restore the eyelid to its normal shape. You may have to be referred to a specialist to have this done, depending on how severe things are and for the majority of operations this is very successful.

Should I breed from stock that has been affected?

It's probably wise not to breed from any dogs that have had to have surgery for ectropion. This will avoid their puppies having similar problems.

Gastric dilatation-volvulus or bloat

Gastric dilatation-volvulus is sometimes known as "bloat" and happens when a dog's stomach becomes dilated or swollen with gas. When this happens, the stomach can twist over on itself and cause very serious problems.

How does a dilated stomach happen?

We know very little about the cause of this condition, but it's thought to be caused by the dog eating a big meal and drinking a lot of water after strenuous exercise. This can also happen at night when the dog can swallow lots of air while resting.

The bloating and build-up of gas can disrupt the normal functioning of the stomach and cause even more fermentation and gas to develop. In serious cases, the bloating can cause the stomach to twist in on itself, blocking the exit and entrance. This twisting of the stomach is called gastric torsion.

Is the condition serious?

Yes. If the stomach twists on itself, this is an emergency and your dog will need urgent vet treatment. Usually this will happen 2-3 hours after eating a meal.

Which breeds are more prone to the condition?

Large breeds with deep chests are much more prone to getting a dilated or twisted stomach. This includes German Shepherds, Great Danes, and Setters. However, small, elderly dogs like Dachshunds often get a dilated stomach without the dangerous side effect of torsion.

What signs should I look out for?

The bloating of the stomach pushes out the rib cage at the back end of the dog. This is more visible on the left side of the dog. In fact, if you gently tap on the swelling just behind the last rib, it will produce a hollow sound.

You should also look out for these serious signs:
- Breathing difficulties caused by the swollen stomach pressing on the diaphragm
- Pressure on the larger blood vessels can cause poor circulation, and the dog might go into shock
- The dog might collapse, lying on one side

How will I know whether the dog's stomach is just dilated or whether it has twisted on itself?

It's very difficult to tell. You should take your dog to the vet as soon as you can, and they will take an x-ray to see it the stomach has twisted.

How can the condition be treated?

It's vital that you get your dog seen by a vet as soon as you can. The vet will want to reduce the pressure on the stomach and vital organs and to do this they might insert a tube, or even pass a needle through the skin straight to the stomach. To treat the shock, your dog will probably be given fluid with a drip. Lastly, the twisted stomach will need to be operated on and returned to its correct position. This surgery is quite complex and comes with a 15-20% mortality rate.

Is there any way to prevent this condition?

Firstly, you should pay very close attention to your dog's diet and exercise. Your vet should be able to tell you if there are any foods or feeding times that should be avoided.

There's also a special procedure that can help prevent the stomach twisting in on itself, called a Gastropexy. This is where the stomach is surgically attached the body wall, preventing the twisting but, unfortunately, not the bloating.

If you have any questions about this condition, don't hesitate to contact the team at Wellpets and we'll do our best to help.

Glaucoma

Glaucoma in dogs occurs when the eye's natural pressure (called intraocular pressure) is raised to abnormal levels. This usually happens when the eye's normal drainage of fluids (aqueous humor) is inadequate. Here are some things you should know about Glaucoma and what can be done about it.

What is primary glaucoma?

Primary glaucoma happens in an otherwise healthy eye. Breeds like Basset Hounds, Springer Spaniels and the Flat Coated Retriever are more prone to developing it. Abnormalities in the dog's anatomy can often be a cause.

What is secondary glaucoma?

This is glaucoma that has happened as a result of a recent infection or injury to the eye. It's more common than primary glaucoma. The normal drainage of the eye can be blocked by a number of things, including:

- A severe infection or inflammation which produces scar tissue or debris
- A dislocation of the lens, where it falls forward and blocks the drainage angle
- Tumour
- A large blood clot
- A damaged lens that is leaking proteins

What signs should I look out for?

The most common signs of glaucoma include:

- A partially closed eyelid
- Shying away from being stroked on the affected side of the face
- Watery discharge from the eye
- Depression
- A swollen eyeball
- The whites of the eyes become red

- The clear part of the eye becomes cloudy
- The dog is having problems with eyesight

These symptoms can happen suddenly (acute glaucoma) or they can develop quite slowly over time (chronic glaucoma). It's important to check your dog's eyes regularly for any of the above signs, because the symptoms can be present for a long time without there being any visible discomfort. Acute glaucoma is considered to be an emergency, so take your dog to the vet immediately.

How will the vet know if it's glaucoma?

Your dog's eyes will be examined with special instruments, internally and externally. The vet will measure the extent of the pressure on the eye with a technique called tonometry. There's a chance you might have to be referred to a veterinary eye specialist to do this.

How is glaucoma treated?

Specialist drugs will be prescribed that will reduce the pressure on your dog's eye as quickly as possible. The eye will need extensive examination to see if there's a cause for the glaucoma which needs to be treated, for example a tumour or a slipped lens. Pain relief may well be needed to ease your dog's discomfort. In severe cases, a dog might need surgery to reduce the pressure on the eye and remove the cause of the blockage.

What are the risks?

Glaucoma is a serious eye problem and it can cause blindness if left untreated. Sometimes the eye will need to be removed completely to avoid infection.

The best way to avoid these complications is to spot and report any symptoms as early on as possible. Dogs that are successfully treated for glaucoma will probably need to have follow-up eye examinations throughout their lives to be sure the condition doesn't come back.

Heart failure in dogs

Heart failure happens when the heart is no longer able to maintain enough circulation to meet the needs of the body. It usually describes the failure of the heart muscle itself, either on the left or the right of the heart. Here, we'll go through some signs of heart failure and what you can expect if your dog suffers from it.

Is heart failure the same as a heart attack?

Not strictly. In dogs, heart failure can cause a sudden collapse and even death, much the same way as a heart attack. However, a heart attack is slightly different because it involves the death of the cells in the heart muscle and a blockage of the heart (coronary) vessels. Dogs don't usually suffer from heart attacks, although they have been known to happen.

What is mitral valve disease?

Mitral valve disease is the most common cause of heart failure. The mitral valve stops blood from flowing back into the atrium when the heart contracts. This valve has to withstand a lot of pressure, and when a dog gets older it starts to weaken and leak, which causes a backflow of blood. This backflow can be heard with a stethoscope and is called a mitral murmur.

Is it serious?

Over time, the condition can worsen and make it more difficult for the heart to pump blood. This can happen months or years after the first signs of a murmur have been noticed.

How do I know if my dog has a heart problem?

Your dog will be less able to exercise and will get very out of breath when they do. Over time there is a build-up of fluid in the lungs and this means the dog will develop a cough, as if it is trying to clear its throat. It's a good idea to reduce exercise when this happens and if

53

your dog is obese, try and help them lose a bit of weight. This should help ease the symptoms.

Is my dog about to collapse and die?

Your dog won't necessarily die from this kind of heart failure, but over time it can develop into more serious heart problems like congestive heart failure.

How is this problem diagnosed?

The vet will listen to your dog's heart with a stethoscope. X-rays will be taken and these will show the lungs as well as the size and shape of the heart. To see if there are any other underlying health conditions, blood and urine tests will normally be carried out.

A special scan (an electrocardiogram) to monitor the electrical activity of the heart will be done to see if there are any unusual rhythms in the heart. An ultrasound can also be helping in watching the con-tractions of the heart. These tests can be expensive, so it's important to discuss them with your vet first, especially if you don't have pet insurance.

How can the condition be treated?

Although we can't cure heart failure completely, lots of drugs are available which will control the condition and make life easier for your dog. These include:
- Diuretics
- Specialist drugs that can actually improve the contraction and rhythm of the heart
- Drugs that can dilate the arteries and ease the pressure on the heart valve

What's the prognosis?

This really depends on how advanced the problem is and how soon you can get treatment. With the right care and attention, lots of dogs have a good quality of life for several months or even years to come.

Heartworm

Heartworm is a worldwide problem and is prevalent in Southern Europe. Dogs that have travelled to affected areas or are imported into the UK are particularly at risk. Here is some useful information you should know about heartworm and how it can affect your dog.

What causes heartworm in dogs?

As the name suggests, heartworm is when a particular kind of worm called Dirofilaria immitis is found in a dog's heart. Usually this will be in the right side of the heart and the nearby vessels in the lungs.

These long, slender worms can be up to 30com long, with females being twice as long as males. A severe case of heartworm could see a dog having up to 300 worms at a time.

How does a dog get heartworm?

The larvae (the immature stage of the worm) is transmitted when an infected mosquito bites the dog. After a period of time, these larvae develop into worms which end up in the dog's lungs and heart.

What are the signs that my dog might have heartworm?

Your dog won't show any signs of having heartworm for at least two years after being initially infected. The most common signs are:
- Weakness during exercise
- Coughing
- Weight loss
- Heart failure on the right side of the heart
- Vital organs such as liver and kidneys can also be affected
- Jaundice
- Anaemia
- Occasionally, sudden death can occur

The symptoms above can be linked to other common illnesses, so your vet will only know for sure by testing your dog's blood for the presence of worms and larvae. Looking at the heart through an x-ray, ultrasound or ECG will also confirm suspicions.

What treatments are available?

There are lots of side effects associated with the treatments for heartworm. In a lot of cases, prevention is better than cure.

How can I prevent my dog getting heartworm?

If you're travelling with your dog, check beforehand to see if your destination is one affected by heartworm. Then, start preventative treatment well in advance of your holiday, at least 3-4 weeks before you leave. Follow the instructions that come with the worming treatment. They will usually ask you to continue treatment for a month or so after your return. If you've already been abroad with your dog, and you visited a place affected by heartworm, you should contact your vet regardless of whether your dog shows any symptoms.

As symptoms can take two years or more, your best course of action is to get a diagnosis before this, as early as possible. Treatment is a lot quicker and easier in the earlier stages of heartworm.

Horner's syndrome

Horner's syndrome is quite a common neurological disorder which affects the eye and facial muscles. It's a condition that usually comes on suddenly. Here is some useful information about Horner's and what to do if you think your dog might have the condition.

What are the signs of Horner's syndrome?

The main signs to look out for are:
• Drooping eyelids

- A sunken looking eye
- The third eyelid in the inner corner of the eye will be prolapsed across the eyeball itself and the eye will be more inflamed than the other eye
- The pupil is constricted

How does Horner's syndrome happen?

Part of the nerve supply to the eye and surrounding muscles is disrupted. Usually, this nerve supply has a long and complex path from the brain to the eye. It passes down the spinal cord and up the neck, past the middle ear and into the eye.

As a result, any number of injuries in these areas can cause Horner's to occur, including a slipped disk, an ear infection, or even a wound in the neck or chest area. It's very common, however, for there to be no known cause at all, and for the syndrome to arise spontaneously ("ideopathic").

Which breeds are more prone to Horner's?

Any breed can get Horner's syndrome, but we do know that ideopathic Horner's is more common in middle-aged Cocker Spaniels than any other breed.

What treatment is available for Horner's?

In lots of cases, once the underlying cause is found, the Horner's syndrome will resolve itself with the dog's natural healing process, usually within 2-4 weeks. Even in ideopathic cases, it will usually resolve itself over time, taking around 8-12 weeks to get better.

Horner's Syndrome looks odd, but it isn't painful for the dog. There are special eye drops available to treat any discomfort which does arise. If there is no improvement after a long period of time, the vet might suggest looking at the nerves and the spinal cord with an MRI scan.

In very rare cases, where the problem doesn't go away, it could be due to brain disease which is very serious. Most cases aren't serious though, and the dog will make a full recovery.

Inflammatory Bowel Disease

Inflammatory bowel disease (IBD) affects the intestinal tract, and sometimes the stomach, of your dog. A lot of dogs with this condition will have an ongoing history of vomiting and diarrhoea. They might lose weight but their appetite will usually be normal. Here are some useful questions and answers on IBD.

What causes inflammatory bowel disease in dogs?

We don't fully understand why IBD happens in dogs, but we know that it happens when the lining of the bowel becomes inflamed and a response similar to an allergic reaction happens. This stops the dog from being able to digest nutrients properly. It's thought that this re-action can happen because of something in the dog's diet, or it might be related to an infection.

How will the vet diagnose IBD?

A blood test will show whether your dog is digesting and absorbing its food properly. It will also show if there's an infection which needs to be treated with antibiotics. The vet may well put your dog on a special elimination diet (for example a high fibre or a hypo-allergenic food) to see if this has any effect. In severe cases, the vet might want to take a biopsy of the tissue in the bowel.

What is the treatment for IBD?

If the special elimination diets don't have any effect, then the problem will need to be treated with medication. The vet might try a few different drugs to see which one suits your dog best.

If the treatment works, then the dog can often stay stable for life and in time, the dosage of the drugs can be gradually decreased. Some dogs might need a change of treatment every few months for symptoms to stay away. A small proportion of dogs just don't respond to treatment at all. In very rare cases, there can be a link to intestinal cancer.

Jaundice

Jaundice is often seen in the gums, ear flaps and eyes of dogs. It's caused by the yellow pigment in the blood and tissues, however, if a dog's ears and gums are usually dark in colour, the yellow won't be visible and the jaundice often goes undetected.

What causes jaundice?

The yellow pigment in the blood is called bilirubin. There are three causes of this:

- Haemolysis: This is the destruction of red blood cells. It can either happen in the blood vessels or the spleen and liver.
- Liver disease: When liver cells are destroyed or bile gets trapped in the liver, it can cause jaundice.
- An obstruction of the bile duct: Bile is an important fluid for digestion. The bile duct can become blocked, causing jaundice.

How can a vet find out what's causing the jaundice?

Usually a series of lab tests will be carried out, starting with blood tests. Once the underlying cause has been discovered, the vet will need to do more tests to get a better picture of what has happened. For example, if the culprit is haemolysis, it could be that your dog has ingested something toxic, or they might have a parasite such as heartworms.

They could even have an autoimmune disease. The blood tests will also be able to show if there is liver disease, another common cause of jaundice. Occasionally, the vet will take a biopsy from the liver to investigate further. The liver disease can be caused by a number of issues, such as:

- Bacterial and viral infections
- Toxic plants
- Certain chemical or drugs
- Breed specific problems with the liver

What causes bile duct obstructions?

If the bile duct is obstructed, it usually causes extreme jaundice in the dog and the yellow colour will be really visible, even on the skin. An ultrasound is probably the best way to look for a bile obstruction because it's non-invasive. Two of the major causes of obstructions include pancreatitis and trauma (injury caused by an accident).

How is jaundice treated?

Jaundice isn't a disease in itself, it's simply a sign that a disease is present. So, the treatment will depend on the illness that has caused the jaundice. It's a very complex problem, but one should look out for if you think your dog is ill.

Lameness

Lameness is when your dog either has a limp or is finding it hard to get around. Pain in the limb or a loose joint is usually to blame. It can happen in dogs of all ages, from young puppies to elderly dogs. Here we'll go through some of the causes and treatments of lameness.

What causes lameness?

Lameness can be caused by an injury or it can be a deformity in the bones. A lot of the causes are age related, for example:

- Puppies with lameness often have a growth defect or an injury
- Adult dogs can have injuries to the limbs, sometimes with no history of an accident

- Old dogs often get a type of arthritis called degenerative joint disease

It's important to note that very often, lameness can happen in dogs without any known cause. This can be something which recurs at certain times, or it might be more persistent.

What treatment is there for a lame dog?

Very strong pain relief drugs called analgesics can be given to ease the pain. These are often used when the vet doesn't know what has caused the lameness. The dose might need to be varied to suit your dog at first. It's a good idea to report any side effects you notice too.

Will my dog be on medication forever?

Not necessarily. Once the lameness starts to improve, the medication can usually be gradually reduced. With non-specific lameness, it's also equally as important to control the amount of exercise your dog gets, to help things to heal effectively.

Leishmaniasis

Leishmaniasis is caused by a single celled parasite found on dogs and rodents around the world. It is transmitted by a sandfly, similar to a mosquito, and alsofeeds on the dog's blood. The fly is very common in tropical and Mediterranean areas. Here are some useful pieces of information on Leishmaniasis and what can be done about it.

Can British dogs get Leishmaniasis?

Until recently the disease was only found in dogs imported into the UK from other parts of the world. However, with the new Passports for Pets (PETS) scheme, lots of British dogs are being taken abroad to places like France and Spain, where the disease is rife. Dogs can get bitten while on holiday and will only show signs of infection once they're back in the UK. It can take 3-7 months for the disease to develop fully once the dog has been bitten.

Some of the main signs of the illness include:
- Dermatitis and skin infections
- Weight loss
- Eye diseases
- Liver and kidney disease

These signs can take years to appear, but when they do, they can sometimes be fatal. Once a dog has been treated, it may still be a carrier of the disease for life and the symptoms may well return at a later stage.

How is Leishmaniasis diagnosed?

Blood or tissue samples are effective ways of diagnosing the disease.

How can I prevent my dog from catching it?

It's important to do your research before visiting any foreign country with your dog. Avoid high risk areas if you can, or simply leave your dog at home instead. If you must visit such an area with your dog, remember that most sandflies feed at night, and will be much more active in summer. Keep your dog indoors an hour before dusk, and an hour after sunrise as these are the most active hours for sandflies. Use insect repellents whenever possible.

At least 3 weeks before you take your dog on holiday, you should start a preventative treatment and your vet will be able to recommend which one to use. Always follow the instructions on the label, and be sure to carry on treatment for at least one month after you get home.

Can the disease spread from my dog to someone else's?

No, luckily the disease will only spread through the sandfly, which isn't found in the UK. The disease can't be spread between humans and dogs either, although humans can still catch it through a sandfly.

The kidneys are the great waste management machines of the body, taking out wastes and toxins from the bloodstream and regulating fluid levels. We all have them, and if they don't work properly then our lives can be under serious threat. The same, of course, goes for dogs, and kidney problems are often an issue, especially for older dogs. The causes of kidney disease are many and varied, ranging from the effects of injuries and cancers to the impact of particular drugs or toxins.

What are the symptoms?

The first symptom to show up is often an increased thirst and more frequent urination (this can also be an early warning sign of diabetes). You might also spot weight loss and general weakness, a lack of energy and a lifeless quality to the coat. Of course, all these things can be signs of other conditions but, unfortunately, if they do indicate kidney problems the disease is probably already quite advanced. For this reason it's well worth getting any elderly dog checked out – particularly if you have noticed some of the warning signs.

What is the treatment?

Unfortunately, it's not usually possible to reverse the effects of chronic kidney disease, but if caught early they can often be stopped from developing further. Your vet will also help you to modify your dog's diet, cutting down on the salt, phosphorus and proteins which put a strain on the kidneys.

What about the liver?

The liver is another major organ, as vital to keeping your dog's body on an even keel as the kidneys, and it too can suffer various ailments. The liver has a myriad of functions, not least in filtering toxins from the bloodstream, and as such it is particularly vulnerable to anything poisonous. Viral and bacterial infections too can have an impact on the liver, and there are certain breeds that have congenital liver-related health issues.

Some symptoms which may be signs of liver disease include weight loss and loss of appetite and energy; these are always good reasons for a visit to the vet. The only true tell-tale sign of a liver problem is jaundice, as the eyes, gums and even skin take on a yellowish tint caused by a substance usually filtered out by a properly functioning liver.

Lyme disease in dogs

Lyme disease in dogs is caused by the bite of a tick (usually a "Deer tick"). When this happens, it usually takes a few weeks for the symptoms of the disease to show. In the article below we'll go through some of the signs of Lyme disease and how your dog can be treated.

What are the symptoms of Lyme disease in dogs?

Lyme disease doesn't affect dogs in the same way as it affects people. Where people will get a rash and flu-like symptoms, dogs experience problems and pain in their joints, which usually develops 2-5 months after being bitten. More serious effects such as heart, neurological and kidney problems will only come about in the very late stages of the disease, if it is left untreated, and are rare.

Here are some of the more common signs to look out for:
- Joints are swollen, hot and sore to the touch
- Sudden lameness (may shift from leg to leg)
- Stiffness
- Walking with an arched back or shuffling
- Depression and lethargy
- Loss of appetite
- Fever

How is Lyme disease diagnosed?

There are lots of other illnesses that might cause these symptoms, so tests are very important in diagnosing whether a dog has Lyme disease or something else. Usually blood tests will be carried out to detect the antibodies produced when the dog's immune system is under attack. If these are present, the vet will be able to diagnose. If not, more tests will be needed, for example a special DNA test can detect the spirochete (the bacteria that causes Lyme's) in the blood cells of the affected joints.

How is Lyme disease treated in dogs?

The good news is that most dogs respond well to a course of antibiotics and will make a full recovery. Your vet might also prescribe some anti-inflammatory drugs to ease the pain of swollen joints and to help mobility. It is very rare for the more severe complications to arise and for the illness to be as serious as it is in people.

How can I stop my dog from getting Lyme disease?

The best thing you can do is to try and prevent ticks from coming into your home or garden in the first place.

Here are some useful tips for doing this:
- Use a topical treatment for fleas and ticks on your dog, and apply it on a regular basis. Your vet will be able to tell you which ones are the most effective.
- Carefully check your dog for ticks every day, especially after walks and spending time in the garden.
- You can remove any ticks you find with a pair of tweezers or a sharp pointed object. Make sure to grasp the tick as close to the dog's skin as possible – don't grasp it mid-body or you will leave the head and it will inject more contaminating saliva into your dog. You can also try scraping it off the skin if that works better.
- Be careful about coming into contact with the tick yourself and dispose of it wisely, wearing a pair of gloves.
- Take care to keep the grass in your garden mowed short, to reduce the habitat of the ticks. You can also use a garden insecticide to kill the ticks.

Bacterial growth happens in the small intestine and is a condition that results in a huge increase of bacteria in the bowel. This damages the surface of the bowel so that it can't absorb nutrients properly, leading to what we call malabsorbtion. Here is some useful information about this condition.

Which dogs are more prone to this condition?

German Shepherds tend to have more problems with malabsorbtion than other breeds. They are prone to problems with the pancreas (exocrine pancreatic insufficiency), but can also get malabsorbtion on its own.

What are the signs that my dog has malabsorbtion?

The main signs are:
- Weight loss
- Chronic diarrhoea

What are the causes of malabsorbtion?

A lot of cases are ideopathic, which means that have no known cause. However, a proportion of dogs with malabsorbtion are found to be suffering from exocrine pancreatic insufficiency.

How can a vet tell if it's malabsorbtion or exocrine pancreatic insufficiency (EPI)?

It's very difficult to tell, but specific blood and faeces tests can be carried out. Usually, a dog with malabsorbtion will not have as good an appetite or as much diarrhoea as a dog with EPI.

Can it be treated?

With a long-term treatment of antibiotics, and a special low-fat diet that can be easily digested, the symptoms can often subside. Long-term treatment might be needed if the diarrhoea and weight loss re-occur. Don't hesitate to ask your vet if you have any questions.

Mange (Canine scabies)

Mange is a skin disease that is caused by tiny mites that live on your dog's skin. If left untreated, the mites can cause scabies, which can lead to a severe skin infection that can be very uncomfortable for your canine companion.

How does the disease come about?

Mange is caused by oval shaped microscopic mites. They can be transferred between infected dogs very easily. There are different types of mange depending on the different mites that have caused it. The most common types of mange are sarcoptic mange (caused by the Sarcoptes scabei mite) and demodectic mange (caused by the Demodex mite). It's important to bear in mind that the demodectic mites are naturally present in most dogs, and usually don't cause any harm whatsoever. It is only when these native mites multiply in large numbers on the dog that they can cause mange. In this section, we'll concentrate on sarcoptic mange which is highly contagious.

How does sarcoptic mange affect dogs?

The eight legged mites that cause this type of mange are found all over the world. The males tend to stay on the surface of the skin, but the females burrow into the skin, digging tunnels into the upper layers. As you can imagine, this is not a pleasant sensation for your dog! The females lay their eggs in these tunnels and the eggs hatch, and later mature into more tunnel-digging females, with a life cycle of about four weeks. The result is an infestation which can be seen by the crustiness of the affected skin.

What are the symptoms?

The disease is more common in younger dogs, but in reality it can affect dogs of any age. Look out for the following evidence of mange in your dog:

- Intense itching, with frantic scratching of the skin
- Red streaks in the skin
- Inflammation
- Sores and scabs, with oozing raw skin
- White crusty areas of skin
- Hair loss

The disease is most commonly visible on the ears, elbows, belly, face and legs but if left to spread, it can affect the whole body. For dogs, it's probably the most itchy, irritating skin condition there is. Humans can't catch demodectic mange, but they can catch sarcoptic mange, which causes a red bumpy rash on the skin.

How does a dog catch mange?

Because it's highly contagious, sarcoptic mange can easily be transferred from dog to dog. It's commonly found in dog kennels and animal shelters where there are lots of dogs kept in close proximity to each other. Like fleas, the mites can also infest blankets and sleeping areas where infected dogs have been. So, you might want to bring along your dog's own bedding the next time you take him to the kennels!

What are the risks?

With mange, secondary skin infections are common. These can be either bacterial or yeast and often smell unpleasant. Dogs can also lose weight and their lymph nodes may become swollen. It's important to bear in mind that some dogs won't show any symptoms at all, and their bodies may have produced antibodies which keep the numbers of mites under control. However, these dogs can pass the mites to a dog with a lower immunity who could become # badly affected.

How will the vet diagnose mange?

Some of the symptoms of mange are unmistakable, such as the white crusting on the skin. If in doubt though, your vet can look for the mites with a microscope. This is easier to do if the crusts are still on the skin (and haven't been washed off by a well-meaning owner) as they can be scraped by the vet and tested as samples. The mites can also often be seen in samples of your dog's faeces. The symptoms of mange are similar to those of allergies in dogs, which cause skin irritations too. To rule out mange if there is any doubt, often the vet will give a special mite-killing medication (an acaracide) to see if it has any affect.

How is mange treated?

There are various medications your vet can give which will kill the mites that cause mange. Some of these are medicine and some will be special washes or dips you can use on your dog's skin. It might be wise to use both, since your dog will probably find a bath and a dip very soothing. You'll need to give several doses over a couple of weeks, in order to kill all the eggs and the hatchlings too. The vet might also recommend that you clip your dog's fur short to help with the treatment. They will also advise you to treat all the dogs in your household even if they aren't showing any symptoms.

Can I prevent my dog from getting mange?

As with any contagious diseases, it will help if you can keep your dog away from large groups of dogs. There are drops you can give your dog on a monthly basis which can repel the mites. These are a very good idea if you're going to be boarding your dog in kennels for any period of time. If you're worried, you can spray your dog with a topical flea treatment when you get home from walks where you have met other dogs.

Obesity

Healthy dogs should not have a problem with losing excess weight. So, if your dog is looking chubby then the first thing to look at is the amount of diet and exercise he gets every day. Changes to these two simple things can make an enormous difference to your dog's wellbeing. A dog that becomes obese is much more likely to suffer from poor health and will not have as good a quality of life as a dog with no weight issues.

In general, an obese dog is not a happy one. Obesity is a serious problem because it:
- Causes your dog unnecessary suffering
- Puts strain on the bones and joints, and the respiratory system
- Shortens your dog's lifespan
- Contributes to conditions like diabetes, heart failure, cancer and high blood pressure
- Makes it hard for your dog to enjoy exercise, which should be one of the highlights of his day

It is completely preventable in most cases – your dog would never choose to be obese!

What are the signs of obesity?

Look at down on your dog from above and you should see the outline of his waist clearly, where the waistline turns inwards just after the ribs. If there's no clearly defined waist, it's a sign of obesity.

Next, gently feel for the outline of the ribs beneath the fur, you should be able to feel the ribs without pushing too hard through the flesh. If you can't feel the ribs, your dog is overweight.

A good tip is to regularly weigh your dog so you can keep an eye on his weight and you know immediately if there has been weight gain or weight loss (both can be a problem).

If your dog isn't keen about sitting or standing still on the scales and they aren't too heavy a breed you can pick your pooch up and stand on the scales. Then, subtract your own weight from the final result and you'll be left with your dog's. The alternative is to make a regular visit to your vet and use their purpose built scales, this will be completely free of charge!

A variety of factors can contribute to whether or not a dog puts on too much weight. These include:

- Breeds with a higher risk of obesity - Cocker Spaniel Retrievers, Dachshunds, Beagles, Cairn Terriers, Cocker Spaniels, Collies, Shetland Sheepdogs, and Basset Hounds.
- Older dogs who are less mobile
- Dogs that are neutered, and therefore have a lower metabolic rate
- Dogs with a very inactive or elderly owner, who can't give them the exercise they need
- An owner that feeds treats to their dogs on a daily basis, but then doesn't reduce their main meal quantity

What other causes of obesity are there?

Lack of activity and regular exercise is a huge factor in obesity. So, too, is diet. But there are some health conditions that cause weight gain too.

These include:
- Hypothyroidism
- Diabetes
- Hyperadrenocorticism
- Neutering

You should always make sure these conditions are ruled out by a vet, before you embark on a weight loss plan for your dog.

How will the vet diagnose obesity?

Your vet will be able to compare your dog's weight with the established standard weight for his breed. He will also palpate your dog's body to see how much excess fat there is. He will rule out any health conditions that may have caused the obesity to develop. Finally, he will also be able to advise you on the right plan of action going forward, including any special dietary measures you should take.

- If your dog is being fed scraps from the table, you should stop this immediately. Some human foods are very dangerous. Fat trimmings from meat, for example, can cause pancreatitis.
- Treats should be only given occasionally.
- If you give your dog a lot of treats in one day, maybe because you are training him or he has had a stressful visit to the vet's, then you'll need to reduce the amount of food you're give him for his main meal that day. This will balance out the amount of calories he's taking in.
- Check that you're feeding the right portion size for your dog's breed, age and size
- Try out different ways to exercise with your dog. Have you tried taking him swimming? What about going jogging or roller skating with your dog? Playing fetch is an excellent calorie burner too.
- If you have a friend with a good tempered, friendly dog, why not bring him along on walks too? Having a companion is more likely to get your dog running around and engaging in important playtime.
- Be careful to increase the amount of exercise your dog gets gradually, and not suddenly, which will avoid putting sudden strain on his body.

Open wounds

Every dog at some point in his life is going to suffer from a cut or a scratch. One of the most common causes of wounds in dogs is having something sharp cut into the soft pads of their feet. Other wounds can be caused by bites from fighting with other dogs, or accidents that happen around the home. Here are a few things you should know about treating these wounds.

Types of dog wound

If your dog has been wounded, you'll need to examine it to see what kind of treatment it needs and whether it's something that needs to be seen by a vet. If you're in any doubt though, do call the vet, who will be happy to tell you whether it needs professional treatment or not. Here are some types of wounds you may see:

Abrasions

These wounds happen when the surface of the skin is scraped off, causing the skin to bleed and become inflamed. Scratching and chewing an area of skin can cause an abrasion, as well as things like jumping over fences, fighting, or being dragged over a rough surface. A lot of abrasions aren't serious, and because the wounds aren't very deep you can usually treat them at home.

To identify an abrasion, look out for:
- A scraped area of skin
- Bruising
- Bleeding or oozing
- Hair loss in the area

Bite wounds and puncture wounds

As the name would suggest, these wounds are caused by sharp objects and teeth that puncture your dog's skin. They might be difficult to spot underneath the fur so look carefully in areas that are bruised or sore to the touch. Bites are particularly harmful as they can transfer bacteria, and they can quickly develop into abscesses. They will need treatment from a vet to properly clean them from the inside.

Look out for:
- Small wounds or holes in the skin
- Bleeding
- Swelling and soreness
- Bruises

Lacerations

When the skin is cut or torn open, it's known as a laceration. Some-times the wound will be a clean cut with defined edges, and other times it can be very jagged and dirty, depending on what exactly caused the cut. Some lacerations can be very deep and can cut into the lower layers of the skin, or even the muscle underneath. If this is the case, and although there may not be a lot of bleeding , you need to get your dog to a vet immediately. He might need stitches to close the wound.

Look out for:
- Broken, cut open skin
- Pain around the area
- Bleeding

Should you bandage a wound?

If the wound is very open and needs to be kept free from dirt and dust, it can be bandaged. Bandaging is also a very useful way to prevent your dog from scratching, licking and biting at the area. It can help to compress the cut and close the flaps of skin on either side. Leg and foot wounds benefit greatly from being bandaged and need to be kept especially clean because they're in close contact with the ground.

Basic steps for wounds at home

Your basic procedure for treating any wounds at home should involve the following steps:
- Stop the bleeding by applying pressure to the area
- Clean the wound – remove any dirt and debris and if necessary, rinse the wound with warm water
- Disinfect the wound – use a gentle antiseptic on the wound and make sure it can't be licked off by your dog
- Bathing in salt water works well, but boil the water first, add the salt and allow to cool down before administering to the injury
- Close the wound if possible
- Bandage over the wound to protect it, use a lint or gauze dressing first, don't use cotton wool as the fibres can stick to the damaged flesh, causing pain when you come to change the dressing.
- If the wound was deep, dirty or very open, it needs to be seen by a vet, so book an appointment immediately

It's very likely that the vet will want to prescribe your dog antibiotics if the wound was dirty, or if it was an animal bite. Your dog might be x-rayed to check for signs of any trauma. He might be prescribed some pain relief and anti-inflammatory medication.

Your vet will also be able to properly clean and dress the wound, in a much better way than you could do at home. He might trim the fur back around the wound to make it easier to treat.

Osteoarthritis

Osteoarthritis is a degenerative disease of the joints, where the cartilage of the joints deteriorates slowly over time. This causes a chronic inflammation of the joints which is very painful and makes your dog less mobile. As with people, it's usually found in elderly dogs.

Is osteoarthritis different to arthritis?

Yes. Arthritis is a general inflammation of the joints, whereas osteoarthritis is a specific condition where the joint cartilage deteriorates over time.

What are the symptoms?

If you notice that your dog is moving around at a slower pace, and that he seems stiff, then it's time to get him examined because he could have osteoarthritis and might be in a lot of discomfort.

Look out for the following signs:
- Lameness
- A stiff walk, stiffness in the morning, and after naps
- Less able to exercise, and less active than usual
- Less able to get up or down stairs
- Symptoms get worse after exercise, long periods of inactivity and during cold weather

Whilst all dogs will eventually slow down and suffer from bone problems with age, some breeds will begin to show signs of ageing sooner than others. In general, dogs that have a poor diet, not enough exercise and lots of illness will age faster, and begin to develop conditions such as osteoarthritis as a result. The good news is that the signs of osteoarthritis are relatively easy to spot and the condition can be managed if it's treated early on.

What causes osteoarthritis?

Osteoarthritis doesn't have a specific known cause, but we do know that things like trauma, wear-and-tear on joints, and defects such as hip dysplasia can contribute to its onset. We also know that obesity is a contributing factor, because the excess weight puts more strain on bones and joints.

How will the vet diagnose osteoarthritis?

The vet will do a very thorough physical examination to look for deformities, swelling and pain in the joints. He or she will also want to know all about your dog's medical history, and whether there has been a recent decline in mobility with stiffness and a reluctance to exercise.

What is the treatment?

Your dog will probably be in quite a bit of pain, so the vet will usually prescribe some pain relief to make things easier, as well as medication to reduce the inflammation. It's also really important that your dog keeps exercising.

He will be a lot less inclined to exercise because of the discomfort, but he needs to keep moving in order to prevent weight gain and to keep his muscles in good shape. Ask your vet if there are any dietary supplements which can help your dog's joints such as vitamins and essential fatty acids. You might be able to switch to a dog food that includes some of these nutrients.

How can I help my dog to live more comfortably?

You should look around your home to make sure it's as comfortable and as accessible as possible for your dog. For example:
- If you don't want him to go through the pain of trying to climb the stairs, you can use a baby gate to prevent him from trying.
- Other small steps around the home could benefit from having a ramp over them.
- Make sure your dog has a super comfortable, cushioned bed to sleep in which will help soothe his aching joints at the end of the day.
- Make sure food and water bowels are raised off the ground so he doesn't have to bend down to reach them.
- You can also try therapies like massage and acupuncture to soothe his pain.

Ovarian cancer

Ovarian cancer can happen to a female dog of any age or breed, although it occurs more often in older dogs that haven't been spayed. If the tumour in the ovaries is malignant, it can spread to other parts of the body which can be very serious. So, it's important to spot the signs early on, and get your dog examined by a vet.

What are the signs of ovarian cancer?

Early diagnosis is extremely important, but it isn't always possible because a dog doesn't always show outward symptoms until the tumour have progressed to a later stage.

With that said, here are some signs to look out for:
- Your dog has stopped coming into heat
- Your dog seems to be having a persistent heat period that is showing no signs of stopping
- A build-up of fluid in the chest or stomach area, with a visible swelling in these areas

- More male dog behaviour which could be due to lower levels of female hormones, . Signs of pain when touched in the affected areas
- Behaviour changes such as depression and lethargy
- Hair loss

How is it diagnosed by the vet?

Your vet will want to know all the symptoms your dog has been showing. Afull physical examination will be carried out, including a palpation of the area where the ovaries are. Blood tests will be indicate your dog's hormone levels. Finally, ultrasounds or x-rays will be used to view the ovaries, check for tumours and see how far the situation has progressed.

What treatment is available?

The treatment your dog will receive will really depend on how far the tumours have progressed. If there is only one tumour, or if the tumours look very small, then there's a good chance your dog can get them removed surgically.

If the situation is more serious, for example, if there are bigger tumours, or if the tumours have spread to other parts of the body, then your dog will not only need surgery but will probably also need some chemotherapy which will slow the growth of the cancer. The vet will also prescribe other medicines, including pain relief to treat any related problems Following diagnosis, your dog will need lots of follow-up appointments with the vet to check that the cancer has not grown or spread.

Can I prevent my dog from getting ovarian cancer?

The best and only way to prevent your dog from getting ovarian cancer is to have her spayed as early on as possible. Usually, spaying involves removing the uterus and ovaries, removing any risk of cancer in these areas at the same time.

Pancreatitis

The pancreas is an organ in the stomach which releases important enzymes needed to digest food. When it becomes inflamed, tender and swollen, the condition is known as pancreatitis. The condition is serious because it causes the enzymes to leak from the pancreas, and any tissue the enzymes encounter is then digested by the body. It's a very painful condition which needs medical attention early on.

What causes pancreatitis?

Middle aged to older dogs are more at risk of developing pancreatitis. There are also some breeds that get the condition more often, such as Cocker Spaniels, Terriers, and Miniature Schnauzers. A diet that's too rich in fat can cause pancreatitis because it leads to too many lipids circulating in the bloodstream. For this reason, it's a really bad idea to feed your dog fatty trimmings from meat and leftovers from your plate. Certain medications can inflame the pancreas, and also some pre-existing medical conditions such as hypothyroidism.

What are the symptoms?

The symptoms of pancreatitis can either be acute, meaning that they come on very suddenly, or they can be chronic, which means they gradually develop over time, and get progressively worse.

Look out for any of these symptoms:
- Loss of appetite
- Weakness, lethargy, depression
- Seeming anxious or distressed
- Vomiting
- Diarrhoea, sometimes with blood in it
- A tender stomach
- Reluctance to lie down on one side
- Fever
- Whimpering or crying in pain
- Collapse
- Hunched position with the chest low and the tail end raised

Any of these symptoms should be reported to a vet as soon as possible, even if they seem to be mild at first.

How will the vet diagnose pancreatitis?

Usually your vet will do a set of blood tests which will show the levels of the enzymes present in the blood. Your vet will also feel the pancreas to see how swollen and painful it is, and he may also look at the pancreas through ultrasound or x-ray.

How is it treated?

If the pancreatitis is only mild, your vet will probably advise you not to feed your dog for about 24 hours, which will give the digestive system a break and should stop any vomiting. Medication can also be given to stop vomiting if needed.

If the symptoms are more severe then there's a chance that your dog might need to stay for a few nights at the clinic, so he can be kept under observation. There, he can be given fluids straight into his bloodstream through an IV drip which will help him feel better and restore the fluids he has lost.

He will be given strong pain relief which should ease his distress. If there is a blockage in the pancreas, which can sometimes happen, then your dog will need surgery to correct it. In very serious cases your dog can be given a blood transfusion which can inhibit the active enzymes that are causing the damage.

Will my dog be ok?

The prognosis will depend on how far the problem has progressed. The first 24 hours of being diagnosed are critical but if your vet can manage to stabilise the condition before any organ damage can occur then there's a good chance of recovery. Once your dog is better, your vet can advise you on the best dietary changes you can make to avoid flare-ups happening in future.

Parvovirus

Parvovirus is a very contagious disease that was only discovered a few decades ago. It attacks the cells that would usually protect the dog's immune system. New strains of parvovirus are being found all the time. It usually affects puppies and adolescent dogs, and is most common in Rottweilers and Dobermans.

How does parvovirus come about?

The virus is spread by contact with an infected dog. When a dog is infected, the virus can be found in its faeces for a few weeks afterwards. Since a lot of dogs do try and ingest faeces of other dogs, the disease can spread quite easily. Parvo can also be found on the dog's fur and its feet. It can infect things like toys, food and water bowls and sleeping areas – anything that comes into contact with the faeces.

What are the symptoms?

The disease has an incubation period of about four of five days. After this, the symptoms can appear quite suddenly and severely.

They include:
- Vomiting
- Diarrhoea (can contain mucus or blood)
- Depression
- Fever
- Dehydration
- Abdominal pain (with a tucked up tummy)
- Sudden loss of appetite

These symptoms can be very serious and should be reported to a vet immediately. Parvo attacks the cells in the bone marrow and the thymus gland which leads to a lack of white blood cells being produced. This destroys the immune system and the intestines. Very young puppies are at risk of dying from the virus.

However, not all cases are life-threatening. If a pup is ill for a few days and doesn't get worse, it means the condition has stabilised and is likely to get better with intense nursing.

How will the vet diagnose parvovirus?

Experienced vets will usually know the signs to look for straight away. Analysis of the faeces will show whether the virus is present or not. Blood tests will also show whether there is a lack of white blood cells which the virus causes.

How is it treated?

There isn't an immediate cure for parvo. However, there are lots of ways that you and your vet can nurse your dog while his own immune system fights off the virus. Fluids are very important to prevent dehydration, and your pup may well be given an IV drip.

As well as this, your dog might be given medicine to treat the effects of the virus which are:
- Anaemia
- Low blood sugar
- Electrolyte imbalances
- Abnormal body temperature

Your pup can also be given drugs to stop vomiting and diarrhoea and to ease any pain and discomfort. Medicine will probably be given by an injection, to prevent it from being vomited back up again.

Lastly, your dog might need a blood plasma transfusion to replenish his white blood cells.

Is there any way to prevent parvovirus?

There is a vaccine against parvovirus which can be very effective in preventing the virus. Ask your vet about it the next time you visit. A booster will probably be needed after about a year. Puppies whose mothers have had the vaccine might have this immunity passed on to them.

Pneumonia

In dogs, Pneumonia is an umbrella term that's used to describe an inflammation of the lungs. It can be caused by bacterial infections or by something foreign your dog has inhaled. It can often present itself at the same time as bronchitis (leading to a diagnosis of broncho-pneumonia).

How does the disease come about?

* Pneumonia has many different causes, including:
* Bacterial lung infections (the most common cause)
* Fungus
* Internal parasites
* Viral infections
* Allergies
* Canine influenza

Pneumonia can also be aspirational, which means it has happened because of something your dog has accidentally inhaled, either a foreign substance or something the dog has vomited or regurgitated that has found its way into the airways.

How does pneumonia affect dogs?

Pneumonia affects the lungs and lower respiratory system of dogs. As well as the respiratory system, it usually also affects areas like the nasal cavities, the throat, the trachea and the bronchi. It's mostly found in very young and very old dogs with weak immune systems.

It can be present in your dog for a while before there are any visible signs, such as breathing problems. If your dog suddenly becomes weak and lethargic, you should take him to the vet, early diagnosis can be a huge help when it comes to treatment.

What are the symptoms of pneumonia?

Look out for the following signs and report them to a vet immediately:

- Rapid breathing
- Noisy, laboured breathing
- Wheezing
- Fever
- A wet cough
- Nasal discharge
- Loss of appetite
- General weakness, depression and lethargy
- Weight loss

If any of these symptoms become severe, don't be afraid to seek emergency medical attention as your dog could be very ill indeed.

Keep calm as your poor dog will pick up on any nervousness and this will make him feel worse. There's really nothing you can do until you've had a proper diagnosis.

How will the vet diagnose pneumonia?

The vet will want to do a full physical examination of your dog. This will include listening to his breathing, palpating the abdomen, and checking for nasal discharge. It might include blood tests to check for infection, and x-rays to look closely at what's going on in the lungs.

How is pneumonia treated?

This depends on how serious the symptoms are and what the initial cause of the pneumonia was. If the symptoms aren't too severe, your dog can be treated at home, with antibiotics to kill bacterial infections. To help with your dog's breathing you can place a nebulizer in your home.

A little bit of exercise, if your dog is up to it, can help loosen any mucus in the lungs. If your dog needs more serious attention, he might need to stay for a few nights at the clinic. He'll be given more intensive care there and can be put under observation. He might also be given some fluids through an IV drip.

A lot of strains of pneumonia are very contagious so you must keep your dog separate from other animals in the house while he is recovering. Give him plenty of fluids throughout the day. Wash your hands after you've touched him and change your clothes before you go to handle any other dogs. Once he's recovered, you should disinfect all toys and food bowls thoroughly. Ask your vet about any vitamin supplements that could potentially help his immune system to fight off infection.

Poisoning

It can be very hard to keep an eye on your dog 24 hours a day, and you can't always be there to supervise what he chooses to eat. However, there are lots of things you can do to prevent poisoning from happening in the first place, and ways to keep potential toxins out of reach of your dog. Even the most seemingly innocent foods can prove toxic to a dog, so you should make sure you and the rest of your family know exactly what your dog is and isn't allowed to eat.

What are the signs of poisoning in dogs?

It's important to remember that the symptoms of poisoning will usually depend on what has been ingested. However, you should look out for the following most common signs:
- Vomiting and nausea
- Diarrhoea
- Drooling
- Loss of appetite
- Internal bleeding – coughing or vomiting blood, pale gums
- Weakness
- Collapse
- Pale gums
- Racing pulse
- Kidney failure – look for excessive thirst and urination
- Jaundice

If you think your dog has been poisoned, you should immediately try to find the source of the poisoning – this will be an enormous help in getting him well again. Take your dog to the vet without delay. If you can, take a sample of the substance with you to show the vet, including any packaging.

Don't try to treat the dog yourself at home – your dog needs professional medical attention. Don't try to make your dog vomit by giving him things like salty water (this could be very dangerous for your dog). However, if any of the toxic substance is on the dog's skin, rinse it off immediately.

How can I prevent my dog from being poisoned?

It can be easy to forget that our canine companions, who will eat almost anything they come across, are delicate creatures and just as likely to be poisoned as humans are. At home, it's a case of being as vigilant as you can, and always being mindful of potentially poisonous substances.

- Keep food cupboards, medicine cupboards and cleaning products completely out of reach of your dog
- Use natural cleaning products if you can
- Avoid using insecticides and pesticides in your garden
- Check all your house plants and garden plants to make sure they're not toxic to dogs
- Don't use rat poison, anti-freeze, or slug pellets
- Don't feed your dog any human foods unless you're sure they're safe for dogs

What are some well-known substances that are toxic to dogs?

Keep a note of these common dog poisons and make sure everyone in the family is familiar with them:
- Chocolate
- Grapes and raisins

- Sweets and chewing gum
- Macadamia nuts
- Peaches and plums, including the stones
- Raw eggs, meat and fish
- Rhubarb, potato plants and tomato plants
- Avocado
- Onions and garlic
- Mouldy food
- Human medicines
- Tobacco, alcohol and caffeine
- Plants like foxglove, primrose, yew, ivy, wisteria, lupin, sweet peas, poppy, chrysanthemum, and laburnum
- Slug pellets, rat poison, insecticide, anti-freeze[1]

Pregnancy

If you think you're about to hear the patter of tiny puppy feet, then it's time to take your dog to the vet for a prenatal check-up. Here are some signs and symptoms of pregnancy and what you can expect in the weeks ahead.

Taking precautions

If you are planning to breed your dog, please first make sure that you're prepared, emotionally, financially and practically, with plenty of time to care for a nursing mother and a litter of pups. You should never take this decision lightly as it really does take a lot of time and effort.

Some things to consider:
- Make sure both parents have the right temperaments to breed from
- Make sure there are no underlying health conditions which could be genetically passed to puppies
- Be absolutely sure that you can provide loving homes for all the puppies, however big the litter
- Be sure that the mother is up to date with all her vaccinations,

worming and flea treatments before she falls pregnant and has a clean bill of health from the vet

Of course, lots of owners find out too late that their dog is pregnant and do not get the chance to take these precautions. Don't be one of these owners! If you don't plan to breed from your dog, get her spayed as early on as possible, and never leave an unspayed female dog unattended with male dogs.

How do I know if my dog is pregnant?

In the first few weeks of pregnancy there are hardly any outward signs, except for maybe a little weight gain. There might be some morning sickness in the third or fourth week, but this is usually rare and only lasts a few days.

- 18 to 19 days: This is the earliest you'll be able to determine whether your dog is pregnant or not. Don't try to do this yourself! Bring your dog to the vet and get a proper examination and an ultrasound. You absolutely must not try to feel your dog's tummy for the presence of puppies, at any stage. This can cause damage and can even lead to a miscarriage. It should only be done by a professional.
- 28 to 30 days: a blood test can be used at this stage to determine whether your dog is pregnant.
- 40 days onwards: you'll notice your dog's nipples enlarge and they will be darker in colour. The belly will also swell at this stage.
- 45 days onwards: an x-ray or ultrasound can show the bone structure of the developing foetuses, and can usually determine the size of the litter. However, the radiation involved in an x-ray is sometimes seen by owners as too much of a risk, and is a decision that shouldn't be taken lightly.
- 63 days: the puppies should be born around this time.

Diet during pregnancy

Your dog is going to eat a lot more than usual when she is pregnant, and after the puppies are born while she's nursing. You need to make sure she has a premium dog food that contains plenty of high quality animal protein. You won't need to give her any additional supplements unless your vet specifically wants you to. Make sure your dog has as much to eat as she likes during this time. Her food portions should only go back to normal levels once the puppies are eating solid foods and her milk is no longer needed.

Exercise during pregnancy

Pregnant dogs still need exercise, as it helps keep their bodies in tip top condition for the birth. Walks are perfect as they are not too strenuous but will keep their muscles toned

Approaching the birth

About two weeks before your dog is due to have her puppies, she should be taken to the vets for a check-up. Now is the perfect time to ask if there's an emergency 24 hour number you can call, in case there are any problems during the labour. Your vet should also give you plenty of advice for the birth itself – be sure to have a pen and paper ready. Now is also the time to organise a whelping box for the puppies to be nursed in. You should also make sure you have some first aid items ready, such as surgical gloves, clean towels, a pair of scissors and some alcohol. You may have to cut the umbilical cords if the mother doesn't do it.

When does labour begin?

A pregnancy lasts around 63 days. At about 56 days, you can start taking your dog's temperature regularly. This will help you to predict when she's about to give birth. Normally, your dog's body temperature will be around 100-101 degrees Fahrenheit. When her temperature drops to about 97 degrees, you'll know that the birth is coming in the next 24 hours.

Prostate problems

The prostate is a gland that surrounds the urethra in male dogs. Its function is to produce fluid that assists the movement of the sperm when the dog mates. There are several problems that can happen to the prostate including prostate cancer, prostatic hyperplasia (when the gland enlarges), and prostatitis (a bacterial infection).

How are prostate problems diagnosed?

Usually, the vet will do a rectal examination to detect any swelling or unusual growth of the prostate. An ultrasound might also be used to look closely at the prostate gland. When the vet suspects cancer, he will also use the ultrasound as a guide when inserting a needle – this is so he can take a biopsy of the cells in the prostate.

What is prostatic hyperplasia?

When there is a swelling or an enlargement of the prostate, it is called hyperplasia. This is caused by a hormonal imbalance and is related to testosterone. It tends to happen in older dogs, although the symptoms can start early and grow over a number of years.

If it's left untreated, the prostate can grow so big that it causes an obstruction of the rectum and make it very difficult for the dog to go to the toilet.

Symptoms of this are:
• Ribbon-like faeces
• Straining to defecate
• Constipation
• Staining to urinate (where the urethra has become blocked by the prostate)
• Blood in the urine

Any of these signs should be reported to a vet immediately as they will more than likely be causing your dog a lot of pain and discomfort. One of the best ways to treat this problem is by neutering, because it removes the source of the problem, the over-production of testosterone by the reproductive organs. Dogs who are neutered will experience a positive change soon afterwards.

This is when the prostate gland is inflamed because of an infection, often caused by cystitis. Your vet will take a sample of the secretions from the prostate in order to diagnose whether there's an infection.

Some of the symptoms of prostatitis include:
- Straining to urinate
- Vomiting
- Diarrhoea
- Fever
- Depression
- Arched back
- Swollen and tender prostate

Your dog will need to be put on antibiotics and these might need to be taken for a long time, because the medication doesn't always reach the prostate at first. If your dog has a chronic case of prostatitis he may have flare ups later on. Again, neutering is a good way to get rid of these problems.

What is prostate cancer?

Prostate cancer is when the cells in the prostate become cancerous and form a tumour. It isn't related to testosterone, so unfortunately it can't be treated by neutering.

Your vet will be able to tell if the prostate is cancerous by looking at a sample of the cells under a microscope (cytology). To treat this, your dog will probably need some chemotherapy and some surgery.

Puppy Strangles

Puppy strangles is also known as juvenile cellulitis. It's usually only seen in young dogs and puppies and is characterised by nodules or pustules on the skin. We don't really know the cause of puppy strangles, but it's thought to be related to a suppressed immune system.

Yes, the condition is more common in breeds like Cocker Spaniels, Setters and Dachshunds. It is very rare for the disease to affect adult dogs.

What are the symptoms?

The symptoms of puppy strangles can come on very suddenly, and might appear to be similar to insect bites or allergies at first.

Here is a list of signs to look out for in your puppy:
* A sudden swelling in the face, particularly the eyelids, lips, and muzzle
* Pustules on the skin, which may ooze and develop into hollows
* Ear infection, with pustules
* Swollen salivary lymph nodes
* Tenderness in the affected areas
* Crusting of the skin
* Lethargy
* Fever
* Loss of appetite
* In rare cases, arthritis
* Hair loss, if left untreated
* Swollen lymph nodes in the throat area, a bit like mumps
* Swelling and pustules will be painful, rather than itchy

How will the vet diagnose puppy strangles?

If the outward symptoms aren't enough to make a diagnosis, the vet can take a biopsy of the puppy's skin. This will help to rule out any conditions that look similar to puppy strangles, like mange for example.

What is the treatment?

Because puppy strangles is thought to be caused by a hyper sensitive immune system, immune suppressants are the main means of treatment. The vet will prescribe a course of corticosteroids to ease the symptoms, and the puppy will usually get better within two weeks of treatment.

Rabies

Thanks to the arrival of very effective vaccines, rabies is very rare in pets these days. It's more commonly found in wild animals like bats, foxes, skunks and other small animals. In the UK, the disease was eradicated in 1922, but the risk is still present from animals being brought into the country, or people who have been abroad and been bitten by animals there, only to return with the disease.

How is rabies spread?

Most commonly rabies is transmitted through a bite by an infected animal. Technically it's also possible to catch it from contact with other bodily fluids from the eyes, nose and mouth, but saliva is the main way it is transmitted. At first, the disease goes through an incubation phase for 3 to 8 weeks, with no apparent symptoms. During this time it travels through the spinal cord to the brain and once the brain becomes infected, the symptoms will begin to show themselves. The brain cells are gradually destroyed and sadly, the disease nearly always leads to death.

What are the symptoms?

In dogs, the symptoms may not present themselves all at once, and some dogs may even show none at all. The first signs are behaviour and personality changes. The dog will seem anxious and will probably want to be alone away from humans and other animals. It might lick the site of the bite wound obsessively. It will later get very restless and agitated, with a very sensitive overreaction to sights and sounds.

After this stage, the dog will get aggressive if approached. He will become disorientated and might get seizures. Paralysis in the head and neck are common and this leads to the dog being unable to swallow, which results in the well- known "foaming at the mouth" syndrome that's associated with rabies. The dog might also have breathing difficulties. At this stage, he is very close to death. Some owners might mistakenly think that the drooling is because their dog has something lodged in his throat and will try to get it out. This can lead to them being bitten or infected or both!

How is rabies diagnosed?

Rabies is very difficult to diagnose in the early stages. In fact, with dogs the only real way to know for sure is to analyse the brain cells in a laboratory after the animal has died. In people, tests can be done while the person is still alive and in rare cases, if it's caught soon enough, the person can be treated successfully.

Vets usually have to diagnose rabies on a presumptive basis, based on the physical symptoms and the history of being bitten. Dogs with a suspected case of rabies might be quarantined so that they can be kept under observation, and so they don't infect other animals and humans. If the vet is really sure that it is rabies he will probably want to have the dog put down, to minimise the risk of infection and to stop the dog's suffering. There is no treatment available that will save a dog.

How can I prevent my dog from getting rabies?

In the UK, the risk of your dog getting rabies is extremely low. However, a good way to protect your dog is to have him vaccinated. This is a really good idea if you're planning to travel abroad with your dog to parts of Europe where rabies might be more prevalent. If you're travelling to a high risk area, you should reconsider taking your dog with you. There are plenty of good quality dog kennels which can take him while you're away.

You can also minimise the risk by supervising your dog at all times, and not letting him roam free where there are wild animals. If he is bitten without you knowing it, you'll have no way to tell if there's a risk of infection, so do be vigilant. If your dog is bitten by another animal, bring him to the vet and have the wound cleaned thoroughly. Then, put him under close observation to check for signs of the disease.

Red eye

Red eye (or pink eye) is sometimes also known as conjunctivitis. It's characterised by a red or very pink inflamed eye which looks very sore and is very irritating for your dog. In this condition, the tissue lining the eyelids can be inflamed as well as thc whites of the eyes, known as the sclera.

What are the symptoms of red eye?

The symptoms you'll see in your dog's eyes will depend on the exact cause of the red eye. The conjunctiva, which is the tissue that lines the eyelids and connects the eyeball to the eye, will be very red and inflamed. Typically, you'll notice it by seeing a difference in the other, healthy eye. The redness is caused by the blood vessels in the eye becoming enlarged and by a build-up of fluid, causing a weeping effect where there is discharge coming from the eye. In general look out for the following:

- Watery discharge, usually a sign of an allergy
- Yellow or greenish discharge which is a sign of infection
- Pus coming from the eye – this can also be a sign of "dry eye" which is when the tear ducts become blocked
- Squinting or a half closed eye is also common
- The dog might paw at his eye or rub his face on the carpet to cope with the irritation

Is conjunctivitis serious?

Normally, these eye conditions are not serious, but they do need treatment from a vet, firstly to stop your dog's pain and discomfort and secondly to avoid any complications which could lead to the delicate eye structures being damaged. If the condition is left untreated the dog's eyesight might be damaged as the infection progresses. Ulcers can develop on the cornea. In very bad cases that have been left untreated, the eye can become so damaged that it might have to be removed surgically.

Are there any other conditions that case conjunctivitis?

One thing to be wary of is that conjunctivitis can be a symptom of canine distemper, which is a very contagious disease. Look out for any other symptoms in your dog like fever, loss of appetite, a discharge from the nose and coughing. Report these to a vet as soon as you can and keep other dogs and animals away from your dog.

How will the vet diagnose conjunctivitis or red eye?

The vet will observe your dog's eye closely. He might want to take a sample of the discharge from the eye to check for infection. He'll also do a full physical examination to make sure there are no signs of other illnesses such as distemper.

What is the treatment?

Usually a special course of eye drops can be prescribed that will be applied straight to your dog's eye. If there is quite an advanced in-fection your dog might need to go on some antibiotic tablets to clear things up. If the red eye is caused by an allergy then the vet might suggest some medication to cope with it, such as anti-inflammatory medicine.

It will probably take a week or two for your dog's eye to recover fully. If there's an allergy, you'll need to find out what the cause is (dust, pollen, mould, cleaning detergents etc.,) and eliminate it from your dog's environment as best you can.

Ringworm

Contrary to its name, ringworm is actually a fungus rather than a worm. It's called ringworm because of the ring shaped red mark it leaves on your dog's skin. The disease is caused by three different types of fungus, Microsporum canis, Microsporum gypseum, and Trichophyton mentagrophytes. All sorts of animals can get ringworm from dogs to humans, rabbits, cats and even hedgehogs.

How does ringworm come about?

Ringworm is more common in puppies and young dogs, and is seen as a single ring shaped lesion. It's contagious, so if your dog has it you will need to wear gloves until the fungus has cleared up. Usually, the fungus gets through the skin where there is a cut or a scratch - it wouldn't normally be able to penetrate unbroken skin. Lots of animals can be ringworm carriers with no outward symptoms. However, it can be easily transferred to dogs by grooming brushes and shared equipment.

What are the symptoms?

The ringworm fungus causes a ring shaped mark on the skin with hair loss. In the centre of the ring, the fur often grows back darker. The skin around these marks will look sore, broken and inflamed and the fur will be in short tufts. It can be itchy and crusty, sometimes becoming infected. Usually, ringworm is found in areas like the tail, paws, face and tips of the ears.

How is ringworm diagnosed?

Ringworm can be seen by shining an ultraviolet light on the area, if ringworm is present the area will glow. Usually though, the ringworm mark on the skin is easily recognised because of its characteristic shape. Other tests that your vet can do, if he is in any doubt, include examining a fur or skin sample for the presence of fungus.

He can also take a culture and see if it grows into fungus in the laboratory (although this takes a few weeks). Besides ringworm, the hair loss might be a sign of mange or another skin infection, so it's important to rule these out, as they will need very different treatments.

How is it treated?

The vet will be able to clip the fur around the affected area and will then apply a special anti-fungal solution which should kill the fungus. The vet can prescribe anti-fungal medication in tablet form, as well as cream to apply directly to the area. At home, you'll need to clean your house thoroughly to remove the fungal spores.

It's wise to keep any other pets away from the infected dog. Wear gloves when handling your dog, so you don't catch the disease. After vacuuming your house, throw out the vacuum bag as it will contain the spores which you don't want to spread. Don't forget to pay special attention to your dog's bedding and the areas it spends a lot of time in. The ringworm itself can take up to four months or more to subside, so be prepared to be vigilant and particularly clean around your home during this time.

Roundworms

Round worms are very common parasites that live in a dog's intestines. As their name suggests, they are round and pale coloured, almost like spaghetti. The medical term for these worms is "ascarids" and when a dog is infected it is known as "ascariasis".

How does a dog catch roundworms?

A puppy can catch roundworms from its mother while still in the womb, as the worms can travel through the placenta. The worms can also be transmitted through the mother's milk once the pups are born. Dogs can also become infected by ingesting the roundworm eggs, which are very hardy and can survive in the soil for a long time.

If they eat an infected animal such as a rat or a mouse that has the worms, they can become infected with the worm. Finally, if your dog eats faeces of another dog or animal, he can catch the worms as they are often present in stools.

How do roundworms affect a dog?

The roundworms tend to live in the intestines where they feed off the nutrients your dog is digesting. They can grow up to 7 inches long and can lay up to 200,000 eggs in a day. When a puppy ingests eggs, the larvae hatch in the stomach and make their way into the respiratory system. The pup coughs them up, and swallows them again, and this is how they find their way into the intestines, where they live normally. Once a puppy is about 6 months old, it will usually develop a resistance to the worms, meaning that they don't fulfil their life cycles. Instead, they lie dormant in the body in an "encysted" state where they are protected from the dog's antibodies and from most worming treatments. The dormant larvae wake up again when a female dog is pregnant, and this is when they migrate to the puppy through the placenta. For this reason, it's essential for any female who is about to fall pregnant to have a very thorough worming treatment. Even then, there is no guarantee that the pups will be safe.

What are the symptoms?

In adult dogs, there are rarely any symptoms at all because the worms are lying dormant in the body. In puppies though, you might notice vomiting and diarrhoea. You might be able to see the pale coloured worms in the faeces or the vomit. If a roundworm infestation gets really bad, it can make puppies very ill and can even be fatal.
Look out for:
- A pot belly
- Weight loss
- Diarrhoea and vomiting
- A dull coat
- A puppy that is generally not thriving, or growing very much
- Anaemia
- Coughing

How will the vet diagnose worms?

Usually the vet will do something called a faecal flotation, where the worms can be detected from the stools.

What is the treatment?

There are lots of worming treatments available and your vet will prescribe the one that's most effective. The worming treatments can only kill the adult roundworms, so you will need to do repeat treatments every two weeks or so to make sure all of the larvae that hatch are killed too. Your vet will tell you how long the treatment needs to go on for, as each case tends to be different. If your dog is pregnant, you need to tell your vet as soon as possible before you start any worming medication. The vet will be able to advise you on how to worm both the mum and pups.

Is there anything I can do to prevent worms?

As an ongoing preventative measure, you should put your dog on a monthly parasite control medication which will kill a range of parasites including worms. You should also be sure that your dog's mess is always cleaned up immediately, and try and avoid your dog coming into contact with other dogs mess.

Can I catch worms from my dog?

Humans can be infected by the larvae of roundworms. It's especially common for children who play in the soil, and who might not practice the best hygiene, to get infected. The worms can't grow into adults in people but the larvae can migrate to different parts of the body and in serious cases they can cause organ damage. Dog (and cat) owners should be especially vigilant when their kids are playing near soil and dog mess.

Salmonella

You might be surprised to learn that your dog can also catch salmonella, despite the fact that he seems to have a strong stomach and an appetite for eating almost anything. Salmonella is a type of bacteria that can live in the stomach without causing any harm. The "friendly" bacteria in the stomach usually keeps the salmonella at safe levels, so it does not normally cause illness. It is only when your dog's immune system is low, or it is exposed to very high levels of salmonella, that it will lead to illness.

Salmonella is often spread through contact with the faeces. This is bad news for the many dogs who have been known to eat other animal's faeces whilst out on walks. It's also very common for it to affect dogs who are kept in large groups, for example in shelters and kennels, where the conditions aren't very clean.

Birds, rodents and reptiles are carriers of the disease and it can be spread easily between animals. Sometimes, a dog that is taking antibiotics will be more at risk of salmonella because the antibiotics kill all the bacteria in the stomach, including the good bacteria that help fight off salmonella normally. Feeding your dog raw meat is also a risk factor, as it can contain high levels of the bacteria which would normally be killed off in the process of cooking.

How does salmonella affect a dog?

The salmonella bacteria usually lives in the intestines, hence being spread by the faeces. It causes severe diarrhoea and in extreme cases it can actually migrate into the animal's blood stream and cause blood poisoning. It can also cause a pregnant mother to lose her puppies.

What are the symptoms?

The symptoms of the salmonella will depend on how serious a case of poisoning it is. Some well- known signs include:
- Diarrhoea or mucus in the faeces
- Lethargy
- Vomiting
- Shock
- Loss of appetite
- Weight loss
- Dehydration
- Vaginal discharge
- Swollen lymph nodes
- Rapid heart rate
- Fever (in serious cases)

Sometimes a dog will have recurring bouts of diarrhoea with no visible explanation, which can come and go over a period of a few weeks. When this happens, salmonella is one of the diseases that should be ruled out.

How is salmonella diagnosed?

As well as assessing the physical symptoms, testing your dog's faeces for the presence of the bacteria by your vet will give a definite diagnosis. .

What is the treatment?

If there are no complications such as blood poisoning, then your dog can be treated at home. A lot of the treatment will involve simply nursing him whilst his body fights off the bacteria.

This should include plenty of water to replenish the fluids lost from diarrhoea and to flush out the system. The vet might also suggest that your dog has no food for a day or two, to help the stomach recover.

How can I prevent my dog from getting salmonella?

Here are a few things you can do to limit the risk of salmonella poisoning:
- Keep your dog's food very fresh, in a sealed container where rodents can't get to it
- Thoroughly cook all "human" foods before giving them to your dog
- Keep your dog away from all reptiles as they are carriers of salmonella
- Train your dog not to eat faeces whilst out on walks, give him treats to distract him
- When your dog rolls in faeces, wash him thoroughly as soon as you can
- Keep all your dog's feeding bowels clean and disinfect them regularly

Shock

A dog that is going into shock is having a medical emergency that needs immediate attention. Shock can be caused by a number of things, from injuries and accidents to poisoning and allergic reactions.

If it isn't treated, it can cause irreversible damage to the dog. You should familiarise yourself with the signs of shock for future reference, and always remember to check for signs of shock when any medical issues occur.

What are the symptoms of shock?

The very first signs of shock are often hard to spot. Your dog might suddenly become very anxious or excited, or in some cases they will suddenly become very subdued. The main symptom to look out for early on is a heartbeat that starts to speed up rapidly.

Later on as the shock progresses, the pulse will still be rapid but it will become very weak and might be difficult to detect.

Look out for these other signs:
- Very pale gums that can have a bluish tinge, and look like they're turning blue
- A very low temperature, well below 100 degrees Fahrenheit which is the normal body temperature of a dog
- Changes in breathing – either very shallow or very deep
- Glazed, unfocused eyes

What is happening when a dog goes into shock?

When a dog goes into shock they basically have extremely poor circulation which leads to a loss of oxygen supply to the vital organs and tissues, including those in the respiratory system. The reason that the heart rate is so rapid is because it is trying to compensate for the sudden loss in blood flow. If these symptoms go on for too long they can be life threatening.

Here are some situations where you should look out for the symptoms of shock:

- After a fight with another dog
- A car accident
- A fall
- A blow from a heavy instrument
- Poisoning
- Severe insect bites, or allergy to bites
- Severe vomiting or diarrhoea
- A bad burn
- An allergic reaction
- A reaction to a certain medication or vaccine

What to do if your dog is in shock

You'll need to say calm, think on your feet and act quickly. If your dog is having trouble breathing you should give him CPR. All dog owners should familiarise themselves with canine CPR techniques as a rule, for any life threatening situations that might arise. Secondly, try to stop any bleeding as quickly as possible by applying pressure to the area and bandaging if necessary. Thirdly, put a blanket over your dog to keep them from losing any more vital body heat.

- Do not try and move your dog, or make him walk
- Don't try to give him any liquids as he could choke
- Don't give any sort of medication unless your vet has been on the phone and has advised you to do so

After you've performed the steps mentioned above, you should call your vet for advice. Don't waste a minute of time at this point as every second is vital to your dog's survival.

Skin cancer

Believe it or not, your canine companion can get skin cancer too, despite the fact that he has a thick fur coat to shield him from the sun. In fact, the skin is the most common site where tumours are found in dogs. For this reason, you should always be aware of any new growths, lumps or bumps that appear on your dog. A good way to do this is to incorporate regular checks into your normal grooming sessions.

How does skin cancer come about?

There are certain areas of a dog's body that are more exposed to the sun, such as the nose and the pads of the feet which aren't covered in fur. Dogs with very short hair and pale fur are more at risk of sun exposure too. However, not all cases of skin cancer are caused by harmful UV rays. Chemicals, viruses, hormonal imbalances and genetic factors can also cause skin cancer in dogs.

How does skin cancer affect dogs?

Not all cases of skin cancer are fatal, but some are. The tumours themselves can be benign (not harmful) or malignant (harmful). The malignant tumours can spread the cancer to other parts of the body if left untreated. Your vet will be able to tell the difference between cancerous and non-cancerous tumours. The tumours themselves can vary greatly in appearance. They might look like ulcers, or they might be a patch of hairless skin that's discoloured. In light of this, any un-usual skin changes should be reported to the vet promptly.

What are the symptoms?

Skin cancer tends to happen in older dogs, particularly Cocker Span-iels and Poodles. The tumours themselves can be anything from 0.2 to 10 cms in diameter. Look out for any hairless raised areas in the skin, which are usually found on the mouth, head, neck or shoulders.

How will the vet diagnose skin cancer?

Your vet will do a thorough examination and will probably take a biopsy to look at the skin cells under a microscope. The vet will also do blood tests and urine analysis, as well as looking at the levels of electrolytes in the body. Skin cancer comes in a few different forms in dogs, including:

- Mast cell tumours: These are the most common tumours found on dogs. Although we don't know their exact cause, they have been linked to hormones, genetics and irritants that have come into contact with the skin.
- Squamous cell carcinoma: This form of skin cancer is caused by exposure to the sun's harmful rays.
- Malignant melanoma: These tumours affect pigmented cells called melanocytomas. These tumours develop very quickly and spread to other parts of the body.

What is the treatment?

The vet will probably want to surgically remove the tumour as soon as possible. If the cancer has spread, more surgery will be needed and possibly a course of chemotherapy to slow down the cancer growth. Steroids might also be used. Overall, the prognosis is good if the cancer is caught and removed in time.

Skin problems

It's important to pay close attention to your dog's skin because it can be a good way to spot a number of health problems very early on. Regular grooming is a good idea because it gives you a chance to look your dog over every few days and closely inspect his skin and coat. Here are a few things you should be aware of.

What are the symptoms of skin problems in dogs?

When looking at your dog's skin and coat, watch out for the following signs of illness:
- Scabs and sores
- Hair loss and bald patches
- Red or inflamed skin
- Scaly patches of skin
- Scratching of itchy skin

- Licking or chewing at a particular spot of skin
- Rashes
- Lesions
- Lumps
- Discoloured skin
- Dried blood
- Pus or oozing skin
- Flecks of dirt in the coat
- Rubbing the face against carpets and furniture

What causes these skin problems?

There are many different causes of the symptoms above and most of the time you won't be able to tell what is wrong without the help of a vet. Here are some common skin problems in dogs:

- Parasites: Fleas are the obvious parasite that springs to mind when it comes to itchy skin. Some dogs can actually be allergic to the saliva in flea bites, which causes a lot of irritation and excess scratching. Too much scratching causes the skin to break out in sores and scabs, which can become infected. Dogs can also be allergic to certain flea treatments, making the problem worse. Look out for the "flea dirt" in your dog's skin; these are comma shaped flecks of dirt which turn a rusty colour when dissolved in water. As well as fleas, lice, mites and ticks are also parasites that can be found on the skin and feed off the blood.
- Fungal infections: Fungal infections such as ringworm are also visible on the skin. Contrary to its name, ringworm isn't a worm but a fungus which causes a ring shaped red mark on the skin and patches of hair loss. The shape of ringworm is very distinctive. It's contagious to other animals and humans so it's important to get it treated early on.
- Bacterial and yeast infections: When a dog's skin is irritated and the skin is broken, it can become infected by a bacteria or yeast. This happens especially when a dog is scratching so much that open sores form on the skin. These sores are then exposed to any infections in the dog's environment and they become even more inflamed in the process.

- Mange: Mange is caused by the presence of mites which live on the dog's coat. They burrow into the upper layers of skin, digging tunnels to lay their eggs, which can cause a lot of discomfort and itching.
- Allergies: Certain substances in your dog's environment can cause allergic reactions. Common allergens include pollen, dust, certain plants and weeds, moulds, and cleaning products with harsh chemicals in them. If your dog is allergic to something in your home he will become itchy and his skin will be irritated. The best thing to do is try and isolate the cause of the allergy through a process of elimination. Get rid of each type of allergen one by one until you find a difference in your dog.
- Food intolerances: There could be an ingredient or a chemical in your dog's food that causes him to develop an allergy. This allergy will again be evident in the skin, which will become very itchy. Fillers, colourings, soy, wheat, corn or even certain meats can be the cause of these intolerances. You will need to switch over gradually to a higher quality dog food with less allergens and filler ingredients.
- Stress: If your dog is stressed or in pain he may compulsively lick himself, causing baldness and sore skin. Dogs that are very bored and kept indoors all day might do this too.
- Hormonal imbalances: The quality of the coat, its thickness and the colour of the skin can all change with certain hormonal conditions.
- When to see the vet: You should never try to diagnose a skin condition yourself. Always visit the vet to get a proper examination done. Some skin problems can be signs of underlying health issues elsewhere in the body, and your vet knows exactly what illnesses need to be ruled out. A healthy dog has a sleek coat and supple skin, so really anything out of the ordinary needs to be checked and treated by a vet.

How will the vet diagnose skin problems?

Your vet will do a full examination of the dog and his coat. You'll need to supply him or her all the information you can about your dog's symptoms and medical history. The vet can take a skin biopsy, and can look at the skin and fur under a microscope to detect certain parasites. Blood tests might be carried out as well as testing for certain allergies.

How are they treated?

There are a wide variety of treatments for skin issues, and the one that your vet will prescribe will depend on the skin condition that has been diagnosed. Antibiotics, for example, might be needed to tackle any infections. Topical treatments applied straight to the skin will also soothe it and eliminate infection. Dips and shampoos that are especially made to kill parasites may also be useful.

How to prevent skin problems
- Groom your dog regularly
- Use shampoos that are only for dogs, and contain only gentle, non-chemical ingredients
- Feed a balanced diet with a good quality dog food
- Do preventative treatments for fleas, worms and other parasites on a monthly basis
- Keep your home free from dust and other allergens

Sore throat and tonsillitis

If your dog's throat is sore, there is usually an underling health condition to blame, rather than a single infection in the throat. The inflammation can be part of a respiratory infection, a sinus infection or a disease such as distemper or parvovirus. So, if your dog looks like he has a sore throat or inflamed tonsils, it's important to get him checked out by a vet to see what's causing it.

What are the symptoms?

If your dog has a sore throat you might be able to feel a swelling in his neck, or you may see some inflammation in the back of his mouth where the tonsils are.

Some signs to look out for are:

- Fever
- Coughing
- Difficulty swallowing
- Gagging
- Loss of appetite
- Trying to eat, and then giving up
- Licking the lips a lot

Tonsillitis as a condition is rare in dogs, but when it happens it is usually in smaller breeds. It causes a high fever, bright red tonsils that are more visible than usual, and sometimes white abscesses on the tonsils themselves.

Is it contagious?

Your dog can catch a sore throat infection such as "strep throat" from you or your family, and if so, the infection will usually move to the respiratory system. Usually, the infection doesn't move the other way i.e. your family will not catch a sore throat from your dog.

What causes it?

If there is a lot of coughing and gagging, this can cause irritation of the tonsils which will then make them inflamed. Dental problems such as tartar on the teeth can also cause infections, which spread to the tonsils. If the dog has an infection somewhere else on his body, such as the anal sac, and he has been licking the area a lot, then the infection can spread to the mouth and throat as a result. When tonsillitis happens with no apparent cause, it is called "primary tonsillitis" and this is the type that normally only affects small dog breeds.

How is it diagnosed?

Your vet will do a full physical examination to see if there is illness anywhere else in the body that might be causing the sore throat. He will look at the tonsils and listen to the breathing. He will also check for dental issues. If he suspects there is a tumour in the throat he will need to take a biopsy. Blood and urine testing might be carried out to check for signs of disease.

Firstly, the underlying cause of the tonsillitis must be treated. So, if your dog is coughing a lot then this should be addressed. Or, if there's a dental problem, this needs to be cleared up with some dental work. A course of antibiotics might be needed to get rid of the infection in the tonsils and bring the swelling down. In very serious, severe cases of recurring tonsillitis the tonsils can be removed.

Stomach and intestinal ulcers

The condition that arises when a dog gets a stomach ulcer is called gastroduodenal ulcer disease. This is when an ulcer develops either in the stomach or in an area of the intestines known as the duodenum. These ulcers are basically sores in the lining of the stomach wall which can be very painful for your dog.

What causes stomach ulcers?

These ulcers can be caused by a number of things, including poor diet and stress. They can also be symptomatic of underlying diseases, so it's important to get a full examination and diagnosis from a vet.

Some common causes of ulcers include:
- Medications that irritate the stomach such as ibuprofen
- Allergies
- Ingesting foreign substances and poisoning
- Infections
- Pancreatitis
- Liver and kidney disease
- Addisons disease
- Inflammatory bowel disease

What are the symptoms?

If your dog has a stomach ulcer, it's very likely that he'll be in pain. A classic sign of stomach pain in dogs is a bowing or praying position, where the tail end is in the air and the head and forelegs are down low towards the ground.

Apart from this, other symptoms include:
- Loss of appetite
- Weakness and lethargy
- Weight loss
- Anaemia
- Vomiting (sometimes with blood)
- Rapid heart rate
- Faeces that are black and tarry due to the presence of blood

How are ulcers diagnosed?

A range of tests can be used to find out whether there is an ulcer, and the exact cause of the ulcer. These include blood tests, urine analysis, and taking samples of the faeces to check for any blood.

 An ultrasound or an x-ray can be used to look at the stomach itself, check for ulcers and, if there are any, see how big they are. If the ulcer turns out to be a tumour, the vet will have to take a biopsy by doing a procedure called an endoscopy.

What is the treatment?

The treatment of the ulcer will depend very much on what has caused it. So, the vet will prescribe medication to clear up any infection, as well as bring down inflammation. Special antacid drugs can be used to protect the lining of the stomach, allowing the ulcers to heal. If the dog is very dehydrated he will be put on an IV drip to replenish the lost fluids. If things are really serious, he might need to be kept under observation at the clinic. This can happen if there are complicationssuch as severe infections, haemorrhaging or shock. Sometimes he will need a blood transfusion if there has been a lot of internal bleeding.

During your dog's recovery, and to prevent more ulcers from developing, the vet will suggest a diet that is less likely to cause ulcers. This will be very bland and low in fat. Wet, tinned food rather than dry kibble is known to be milder and less abrasive on the stomach and easier to digest. If any medications are needed for pain, buffered aspirin is best or natural remedies.

Tapeworms

Tapeworms are parasites that are very common in dogs. They can grow to 12 - 18 inches long as adults and live in the intestines of your dog. They don't have a mouth, but instead feed through their skin. Their bodies have special hooks that attach to the walls of the intestine, and are divided into short pearl-like segments.

How do tapeworms infect my dog?

The tapeworm uses two hosts in its life cycle – the flea and an animal such as a dog or cat. When the tapeworm is ready to lay eggs, the last few segments of its body break off and move out of the dog's body along with a bowel movement. You can sometimes see these segments on top of the dog's faeces.

These segments are full of thousands of eggs, which scatter wherever they land. The tiny eggs are ingested by the larvae of fleas, and they hatch inside them and form cysts. The fleas themselves are then ingested by a dog, or another animal, usually during grooming, and the immature tapeworms can then reach the dog's intestines and live out the rest of their days there.

What are the symptoms of tapeworms?

Usually, you will see the off-white coloured worm segments around your dog's bottom or on its faeces; they look like grains of rice and might be moving slowly at first, until they dry. They're quite distinctive but if you aren't sure, try to collect a sample and bring it along in an air-tight container to be analysed by the vet. The tapeworm itself doesn't cause any severe symptoms like vomiting or diarrhoea, so if your dog is experiencing these they are probably due to a separate health problem. Sometimes, if your dog has a bout of diarrhoea at the same time, the long body of the tapeworm might be excreted with the faeces.

This doesn't mean that the whole tapeworm is no longer in your dog's intestines – often the head is left behind and the worm simply regrows.

Lastly, if your dog has fleas then the chances of him having tapeworm is high but if he is free from fleas, it doesn't necessarily mean he doesn't have a worm or two lurking. It only takes a single flea to infect a dog with tapeworms and your dog may well have caught one in his mouth before you even had the chance to spot it.

Are tapeworms harmful to my dog?

The tapeworms themselves won't cause any harmful symptoms, but as they are a parasite and feed off the nutrients in your dog's body, they are still not good for his health and you should get them treated quickly.

How will the vet diagnose tapeworms?

Usually a faecal examination will be done. However, it's important to note that this can be inconclusive. The segments with the eggs may not be excreted in every bowel movement, and you may have spotted them a day or two before you bring your dog to the vet's and not see them again for another day or so. If you are sure you have seen evidence of tapeworm you should have your dog treated, in any case.

What is the treatment?

The good news is there are lots of very effective treatments for tapeworms, and they are perfectly safe for your dog. You should make sure that you use a worming treatment specifically designed to kill tapeworms, as not all worming treatments are able to. As well as this, you should do a flea treatment too. Make sure to treat all the pets in the house to prevent a recurrence.

Thyroid problems

The thyroid is a gland in your dog's body that is located near the wind pipe in the neck. It helps to regulate the metabolism and is controlled by the pituitary gland in the brain. There are two well known problems that can happen in the thyroid: hyperthyroidism and hypothyroidism, both of which we'll explain here.

What is hypothyroidism?

Hypothyroidism is when the thyroid becomes underactive, leading to sluggishness and a slow metabolism. This can happen in two situations. Firstly, the immune system can treat the thyroid as a foreign object and start to attack it. The second form is when the thyroid tissue is replaced by fat tissue over time. We don't know the cause of either of these or why they happen.

What are the symptoms of hypothyroidism?

Almost every organ in the body is affected by hypothyroidism. Here are some common signs to look out for in your dog:
- Weight gain despite eating a normal amount of food
- Lethargy, a lack of energy and a reluctance to exercise
- Feeling the cold more than usual
- A coat that is thinning and shedding hair with balding in places
- Skin and ear infections that are recurring
- High blood cholesterol

In serious cases, hypothyroidism can cause nerve damage and this can lead to lameness, dragging the feet and bad co-ordination. Dogs that haven't been neutered will suffer a loss of libido, and females will stop coming into heat. Eye problems like dry eye (where the eye stops producing tears) and fatty deposits on the cornea can also happen in serious cases.

How is it diagnosed?

The vet will test your dog's blood to look at the levels of thyroid hormones present. If this is inconclusive they will do further testing to rule out other conditions.

Hypothyroidism can't be completely cured, but the condition can be managed with the use of medication, which is designed to replenish the lost thyroid hormones. These tablets will probably be needed for the rest of your dog's life.

What is hyperthyroidism?

Hyperthyroidism is the opposite of hypothyroidism, where the thyroid gland is actually over active, leading to a metabolism which is too fast. This is caused by a tumour in the thyroid which can affect either one or both of the thyroid "lobes". In dogs, these tumours are often cancerous and difficult to treat.

What are the symptoms of hyperthyroidism?

Look out for the following:
- Weight loss
- Increased thirst
- Hyperactivity
- Restlessness
- Problems swallowing
- Swelling in the neck

How is it diagnosed?

Usually a blood test can show whether the dog's thyroid is working normally or not. The test will show how much of the thyroid hormone is in the dog's body. An ultrasound or x-ray might also be used to look at the throat for tumours.

How is it treated?

Often hyperthyroidism is cancerous, so the thyroid itself might be surgically removed if possible. Treatment will be aimed at giving the dog the best quality of life under the circumstances, and keeping the growth of the cancer to a minimum.

Ticks

Ticks are parasites that live off the blood of mammals. They latch on to their hosts and feed from their blood, dropping off afterwards when they have had enough. They can transmit various diseases to their hosts such as Lyme disease.

What do ticks look like?

Ticks can vary in size and colour, and their appearance tends to depend on how recently they have fed and how old they are. They can be as small as a pin head, or as big as an apple seed. When they have fed, they become engorged and will be significantly bigger than usual.

When they are in the middle of feeding on your dog, you probably won't be able to see the tick's legs or its head, making them look quite strange, almost like a pebble. They can be cream coloured, grey or even dark brown. They will usually go for the areas of your dog's skin that are the least hairy, and where the skin is quite thin, such as the face, neck, belly and insides of the legs.

How did my dog get a tick?

If you've been walking your dog in an area of long grass, or somewhere humid like a marsh or forest, then there's a good chance he will pick up a tick as those are the habitats that ticks like best. They often lie in wait on foliage for their next host to come along. It's a good idea to check your dog for ticks after walks, so that you can catch them as early on as possible and get them removed before they transmit any diseases.

What should I do if my dog has a tick?

A tick has to be removed in a very precise way, so that the head and the whole body are removed. Often, the head is lodged in the skin while it feeds and so a well-meaning dog owner will succeed in only removing the body. Because of this, veterinary surgeries get clogged in the summer months with owners who want the vet to remove the tick correctly for them. The good news is that this can be done at home with the right know-how.

Here are some tips:
- Use the right tools. You can buy special tick removers or twisters from online pet shops which are very easy to use. Or, try a tweezers with a very blunt, precise end.
- Be extremely gentle and grab the tick as close to the dog's skin as possible. Don't apply any pressure and this will squeeze the tick and kill it, and you might find the head is still embedded in the dog's skin. The head can excrete toxins, so you want to avoid this by all means. Use a gentle twisting motion to pull the tick away and out of the skin.
- Once you've removed the tick, dispose of it safely, in a sealed container. The last thing you want is for it to find its way back to the dog, or to your family's skin.
- Don't try to scrape or brush the tick away from the skin. It's head and probes might be left behind, leading to infections.
- Don't use your bare hands to remove the tick – always use a tool instead. This will avoid you catching any diseases it might be carrying.
- Don't try to use insecticide on the tick or to flush it out with any other substances. It needs to be physically removed, in one piece, from your dog's skin.
- Don't put off removing the tick till later in the day. You may find by that stage it has moved on to a different part of the body or may even have found a new host. The longer the tick is left on your dog, the higher the chances of a disease being transferred.
- Once it has been removed, wash the area where the tick has been thoroughly with an antiseptic solution.
- If you haven't managed to get the tick removed in one piece, and there is still some left in your dog's skin. Bring him along to the vet to have a look.

There are a few tick-borne diseases that have been known to affect dogs. One is Lyme's disease, which only begins to affect a dog 2-5 months after it has been bitten.

The symptoms to look out for are:
- Joints are swollen, hot and sore to the touch
- Sudden lameness (may shift from leg to leg)
- Stiffness
- Walking with an arched back or shuffling
- Depression and lethargy
- Loss of appetite
- Fever

Babesiosis is another tick borne disease which mainly affects younger dogs and puppies who have no built-in immunity to the illness. It can't be passed from one dog to another, and is only spread by ticks. It is relatively new in the UK and has become a problem since quarantine laws were relaxed and pets began to travel more frequently throughout Europe.

Some of the signs and symptoms of the disease include:
- Depression
- Weakness
- Loss of appetite
- Pale gums, lips, tongue or eyelids
- Fever
- Dark coloured urine

How can I prevent my dog from getting ticks?

The best thing you can do is to try and prevent ticks from coming into your home or garden in the first place.

Here are some useful tips for doing this:
- Use a topical treatment for fleas and ticks on your dog, and apply it on a regular basis. Your vet will be able to tell you which ones

are the most effective .
- Carefully check your dog for ticks every day, especially after walks and spending time in the garden.
- Take care to keep the grass in your garden mowed short, to reduce the habitat of the ticks. You can also use a garden insecticide to kill the ticks.

Tracheal collapse

The collapse of the trachea or windpipe is one of the main causes of airway obstructions in dogs. We don't know why it happens but we do know that a genetic abnormality can sometimes cause the trachea to form a less circular shape than usual, and that this increases the risk of collapse.

How does a tracheal collapse come about?

A healthy windpipe is made from strong rings of cartilage that allow air to travel to and from the lungs. When the wind pipe is weakened and the rings of cartilage collapse, the air only has a small space to squeeze through, you will notice a honking cough or wheeze in your dog.

What are the symptoms of tracheal collapse?

Look out for the following signs:
- A honking cough
- Wheezing and laboured breathing
- Intolerance or reluctance to exercise
- Discoloured gums with a bluish tinge to them

The coughing and wheezing in your dog might be aggravated by all sorts of things in his environment, for example smoke, dust, pollen or even just being overexcited.

Are some dogs more prone to tracheal collapse?

Yes. Smaller toys breeds of dogs such as Yorkies are more at risk. It can happen to dogs of any age but is more common in middle aged to older dogs.

How is it diagnosed?

Usually, the honking cough will be a big sign that a tracheal collapse has happened. If the vet is in doubt he can use x-rays and ultrasounds to look more closely at the windpipe. If this proves difficult, but the vet still suspects a collapse, there are specialists who can perform something called a fluoroscopy which is a way to look at the trachea and how it moves while the dog is breathing.

What is the treatment?

A lot of the treatment will involve helping your dog to breathe more easily. The vet will prescribe cough suppressants and medication to control any inflammation in the windpipe. If the dog is overweight, putting him on a weight loss plan can be a big help to his breathing. In very severe cases the dog will need to undergo surgery and this will need to be carried out by a specialist.

How can I help my dog?

If your dog has suffered a tracheal collapse, there are a few things you can do to ease his discomfort, including:

- Switch from a lead to a harness, which will put less strain on his delicate windpipe area
- Eliminate irritants from your dog's environment that could be causing him to cough and wheeze more
- Help your dog to lose weight if he needs to

Tumours

A tumour is a lump or a growth that can be located anywhere in your dog's body. Tumours can be cancerous (malignant) or non-cancerous (benign). If you think your dog might have a tumour, here are some things you should know.

What are benign tumours?

A benign tumour grows very slowly and doesn't spread to other parts of the body. It doesn't invade or destroy the neighbouring cells. Usually, it can be treated simply by removing it surgically.

What are malignant tumours?

A malignant tumour is harmful and possibly life threatening for your dog. It is cancerous, and needs to be treated as early on as possible before it spreads. The cancerous cells in a malignant tumour can break apart and enter the bloodstream and the lymph nodes, causing cancerous cells to grow in other areas of the body.

Where can tumours be found?

Most tumours are found in older dogs aged 7 years and upwards. The most common places for dogs to get tumours are:
• Skin
• Lymph glands
• Mammary glands (breast cancer)
• Testicles
• Mouth
• Bones of the limbs
• Liver and spleen
• Gastrointestinal tract

What are the symptoms of non-visible tumours?

If your dog has a cancer in the liver, spleen or gastrointestinal tract, for example, the first signs that there is any cancer will be weight loss, vomiting, diarrhoea, a swelling in the abdomen, bloody faeces and constipation.

How will the vet diagnose a tumour?

Lots of tumours can be felt under the skin, but not all tumours are immediately obvious, and some can only be detected through scans

122

and ultrasounds. Your vet will be able to palpate your dog's body for signs of swelling and any unusual lumps or bumps.

What causes tumours?

Very little is known about the causes of benign tumours and why these swellings appear over time. In cancerous tumours, we know that anything that disrupts the normal duplication of cells can lead to cancer. We also know that certain breeds of dog are prone to certain types of cancer. For example, Scottish Terriers have a high chance of developing cancer of the bladder.

Here are some of the common causes of cancer:
- Genetic disposition
- Exposure to carcinogens (cancer causing chemicals such as cigarette smoke)
- Radiation from the sun
- Radiation from x-rays
- Trauma to certain areas
- Certain viruses

How are tumours diagnosed and treated in dogs?

Usually a tumour will be detected by palpating (feeling) the body for unusual growths, and by using scans, x-rays and ultrasounds to check for the presence of growths in the vital organs. Once detected, the vet will want to remove the tumour surgically, if it is possible. A biopsy will be taken to see if the cells are cancerous. If it is cancer then the treatment will usually be a course of chemotherapy and perhaps some more surgery. Medicine such as pain relief will also be used to treat the symptoms of the cancer and improve your dog's quality of life.

Urinary incontinence

Urinary incontinence usually happens on older or elderly dogs and is more common in females than males. As well as this, some breeds, like Springer Spaniels, Cocker Spaniels and Dobermans, are more prone to urinary problems than others. Incontinence involves a loss of control over the bladder, which often leads to accidents around the house in dogs that are normally housetrained. These accidents might be very minor or there can be a large emptying of the bladder.

What are the symptoms of incontinence?

Usually, the accidents that begin to happen around the home are a big sign that a dog has a problem with incontinence. Apart from that, look out for a leaking or dripping of urine from the dog. There might also be obsessive licking of the urethra area.

What are the causes of incontinence?

Here are some of the most common conditions that cause a loss of bladder control in dogs:
• Urinary stones
• Urinary tract infections
• Hormonal imbalances
• A weak bladder muscle
• Prostate problems
• Injuries and problems with the spine
• Conditions such as diabetes and kidney disease, which cause excessive thirst and urination
• Birth defects and anatomical abnormalities

How will the vet make a diagnosis?

As well as examining the dog physically and taking into account his medical history, the vet will also probably do some urine analysis to see if there is an infection in the urinary tract. The vet might also do a urine culture, and may take blood tests. An ultrasound or x-ray might be needed to look at the dog's urinary system in close detail.

Is urinary incontinence a serious condition?

Apart from being very inconvenient and unhygienic, your dog can develop a serious bladder infection if his incontinence is left untreated.

If your dog wets themselves in the night and their fur comes into contact with the urine, then this could lead to a secondary skin infection.

How is it treated?

The treatment your vet prescribes will naturally depend on what has caused the incontinence. For example, if it's an infection, then antibiotics may be needed. Some other possible treatments include:
- Medication that will strengthen the muscle in the bladder
- Surgery to correct any problems with the bladder
- Surgery to remove bladder stones and other obstructions
- Collagen injections
- Hormone therapy
- Pain relief

What should I do if my dog has urinary incontinence?

You should take your dog to the vet as soon as you can to get to the bottom of it, so to speak! As well as this, here are some tips:
- Keep your dog and his surroundings as clean and sterile as possible to avoid infections;
- Give your dog plenty of toilet breaks outside, as many as it takes to see a difference;
- Use something waterproof like a plastic sheet under your dog's bedding, and change his bedding as soon as it is soiled

Urinary tract infections

Urinary tract infections (UTIs) are more common in older female dogs and can be very painful and uncomfortable. It's important to bear in mind that a dog might not show any signs of a UTI at all, possibly because they have a high pain threshold.

So, it's a good idea to keep a close eye on your dog's urinary habits to see if you can spot any problems that may not be immediately obvious. This could save your dog a lot of discomfort later on and could prevent serious complications from arising.

If the dog is showing symptoms, they will usually include one or more of the following:
- Urinating very frequently
- Drinking a lot more than usual
- Straining to urinate, and difficulty passing urine
- Incontinence, with accidents around the house
- Urine that is cloudy or smelly
- Blood in the urine
- Lethargy, depression and listlessness
- Lack of appetite
- Fever
- Vaginal discharge
- Licking around the painful area of the urethra

Don't put off bringing your dog to the vet in the hopethat things will clear up. If left untreated, these infections can spread to the kidneys and can cause blood poisoning.

Which dogs are more prone to UTIs?

Females are more at risk of getting urinary tract infections, and this is thought to be because they have a much shorter and wider urethra. Dogs with existing medical conditions such as diabetes or Cushings disease will also have more trouble with urinary infections. Also, dogs that have a low immune system already, or are taking medications that suppress the immune system, are more likely to get a UTI.

How will the vet make a diagnosis?

At the vets you can expect some urine analysis to be carried out, so you will need to take a sample and bring this in to the vets. The vet will do a full physical exam which will focus especially on the kidneys and bladder. Blood tests might be needed and if the vet needs to take a closer look, he will do an ultrasound to see what is happening in the urinary tract.

If there is just a straightforward urinary tract infection, the vet will prescribe some antibiotics which should clear things up. The dog might need some medication to change the pH (acidity/alkalinity) of the urine. Lots of fluids will be needed to flush out the system, and the vet might want you to make some changes to your dog's diet. For example, wet tinned food contains more moisture than kibble and might be a good way for your dog to get more fluids. If the vet has found any stones or obstructions in the urinary tract, the dog will need surgery to remove them.

Vitamin D poisoning

Vitamin D is a nutrient that is stored in the fatty tissues of the body. It does important work such as regulating the levels of calcium and phosphorous in the body, and helping the body to retain calcium. We also know that there is a strong relationship between vitamin D levels and the health of the heart. If your dog accidentally ingests too much vitamin D, it can be poisonous and make your dog seriously ill. So, it's important to familiarise yourself with the signs of poisoning.

What causes vitamin D poisoning?

Vitamin D is a fat soluble vitamin, which means excess amounts of it are stored in the liver, just like excess fat. A dog can easily be poisoned if the levels of vitamin D build up to dangerous amounts and the liver is overloaded. This can happen under the following circumstances:
- If the dog accidentally ingests rodent poison
- If the dog is given too much of any vitamin D supplement even those meant for dogs
- If a dog is fed a diet containing too much vitamin D

What are the symptoms?

Vitamin D poisoning can be very serious, and the first 72 hours of ingestion are crucial to your dog's recovery. That means you'll have to spot the symptoms as early on as possible.

Look out for:

- Excessive drooling
- Vomiting (sometimes containing blood)
- Increased thirst and urination
- Loss of appetite
- Weakness and depression
- Abdominal pain
- Black tarry faeces
- Constipation
- Muscle tremors
- Seizures
- Slow heart beat

How is it diagnosed?

Your vet will want to know exactly what your dog has ingested, and what symptoms they have been showing. He will do a full set of blood tests to check for the presence of too much calcium and phosphorous in the blood, among other things. A urine sample will also be useful to show whether there are high levels of proteins and glucose.

How is vitamin D poisoning treated?

If the poisoning is reported straight away, vomiting can be a way to bring it out of the system before it reaches the liver. Charcoal can also be useful in these situations. Otherwise, the dog will have to be put on intravenous fluids and maybe some electrolyte therapy. If there is a serious case of poisoning it may cause kidney failure, which will need much more intensive treatment. You'll also need to eliminate all sources of vitamin D from the diet while your dog recovers.

Unexplained weight loss

If your dog is normally a healthy weight and has suddenly begun to shed pounds, and you haven't changed their diet or increased their exercise, then there is more than likely an underlying health condition to blame. You'll need to bring him to the vet for a full examination to get to the bottom of the cause. Don't wait and see if it gets better because there probably is something that needs medical attention, and your dog could be in real discomfort without you knowing it.

About 70% of your dog's body is made up of water. So, it's important to check whether the rapid weight loss is fat or just water. If it's the latter, your dog could have a serious case of dehydration which needs to be addressed immediately. If the dog is losing fat, this can also be serious if left untreated for a long time. The dog will waste away and this can lead to death.

What causes weight loss?

Weight loss is a symptom of a large number of conditions. Sometimes though, it can be one of the following less serious reasons:
- Your dog is eating less because you've changed his diet, and he doesn't like the new food as much
- Your dog is eating the same amount, but you've recently changed his food to something with lower calories
- Your dog, or you have become more active recently, and both are getting more exercise than before
- Your dog is simply getting old and has lost weight as a result of the ageing process

Sometimes though, there is something more serious behind the weight loss.

This could be one of the following conditions:
- Dental problems
- Liver disease
- Kidney failure
- Diabetes
- Cancer
- An obstruction in the digestive tract
- Parasites
- Bacterial or fungal infections
- Pancreatitis

- Pregnancy and nursing

This list isn't exhaustive. Only your vet will be able to tell what has happened to cause the weight loss.

What other signs should you look for?

If your dog has an underlying health problem such as the ones mentioned above, there's a good chance he'll be displaying some other symptoms too. Knowing these will help your vet to make a diagnosis.

Ask yourself some of these questions prior to your visit:
- Has your dog's diet changed?
- Has there been any sort of lifestyle change, such as a new house, a bereavement, a new pet in the family?
- Is your dog showing any signs of the following: vomiting, diarrhoea, lethargy, depression, signs of pain?
- Is your dog trying to eat and then giving up? This could be a sign of a dental problem making it difficult to eat.

How will the vet make a diagnosis?

The vet will have to do a number of tests in order to rule out certain medical conditions. He will do blood tests, urine tests, and a full physical examination. He may want to look at a sample of your dog's stools, and he may also do an ultrasound to see what is going on in the stomach.

What is the treatment?

Because the causes of weight loss are so numerous, the treatment will depend largely on what health problems are at the root of the weight loss. If it's as simple as your dog being off his food, you will need to try out some different foods to tempt him to eat again. If he's on dry food, you might want to try him with a wet, tinned dog food instead. These are often more flavoursome and are easier to digest. You can try warming up the food to make it smell more tempting and adding a chicken broth to it to add to the aroma. All changes to a dog's diet should be done gradually and not suddenly, to avoid any stomach upsets.

Wobbler's syndrome

Wobbler's syndrome is a condition that involves a compression of the spinal cord and the spinal cord roots are compressed. This is not only painful but it can also lead to neurological problems which are evident in the unsteady, wobbly walk that dogs with the syndrome can develop.

How does wobbler's come about?

Wobbler's usually affects the larger dog breeds such as Dobermans, Rottweilers, Irish Wolfhounds and Great Danes. It happens in two ways; firstly, as a result of slipped disks in the spine that can be bulging or herniated. Secondly, it can happen as a result of a badly formed vertebral canal. Both of these issues can lead to the compression of the spinal cord and nerve roots.

What are the symptoms?

- A wobbly walk with short steps and swaying back legs
- Neck pain
- Weakness in the limbs
- Difficulty getting up after sitting or lying down
- Paralysis in the limbs – partial or complete
- Muscle wastage in the shoulders
- Nails that are worn from being dragged

Unless it has been caused by a sudden injury, wobbler's is usually a disease that has a slow, progressive onset. The symptoms usually start in the hind legs and you might notice your dog standing in a hunched position with his head held low because of the pain.

What causes wobbler's?

The exact cause of wobbler's isn't known, but it's thought to be related to very fast growth in some of the larger breeds, where the rapid growth causes problems in the spine. Nutrition is also thought to have an impact, with excess protein, calcium and calories causing issues, especially in Great Danes.

How will the vet diagnose wobbler's?

If you can give the vet any information about your dog's medical history, it will be very useful, especially if your dog has suffered any traumas in the past or if there are any genetic conditions you know of. The vet will do a full physical examination and observe the dog's gait. He will do a number of tests on the blood and urine to rule out underlying medical conditions.

Most importantly, the vet will want to take a good look at the spine and the bones surrounding it. He will do this by taking x-rays and maybe CT scans.

How is it treated?

Surgery is often the best way to treat wobbler's. After on the operation, your dog will need to have his exercise restricted for a few months to help his body to recover. He will also need some physical therapy. If your dog does not have surgery you'll need to nurse him at home, and make it easy for him to get about the house.

In cases where he can't move very much you might need to help him roll over onto his side to prevent him getting bed sores. He might benefit from things like aqua therapy and acupuncture during his recovery. During this time it's important not to try and put a lead on him as this will cause him pain to the delicate area of his neck, which will already be very sore.

Can I prevent my dog from getting wobbler's?

If your dog is one of the large breeds at risk of developing wobbler's, then one very useful thing you can do is to give him supplements that will support his cartilage and muscles, from an early age. Ask your vet what the best supplements would be. Lots of exercise to improve muscle tone is important and of course, using a harness instead of a lead to prevent damage to the neck.

Vomiting

If your dog is vomiting it could be a sign of a number of diseases, conditions or even allergies. You'll have to look closely for other symptoms to know what is wrong, and of course, you'll need to take the dog to the vet if the vomiting has gone on for longer than about 12 hours. Below are some possible causes of vomiting and some useful signs to look out for.

What are the symptoms of nausea?

Signs that your dog is generally feeling nauseous include drooling, licking their lips and gulping or swallowing. He will more than likely not be able to eat or drink anything if this is happening.

When the vomiting does occur, make a note of the circumstances. For example, does it happen after eating? After exercise? Or at night time? How long has the vomiting been going on for? The vet will need to know these things when you see him.

What behaviour should I look out for?

As well as vomiting, you need to check if your dog is behaving in other unusual ways, as this will be a great help when your vet is diagnosing.

Look out for changes in behaviour such as:
- Panting
- Loss of appetite
- Aggression, or not wanting to be touched
- Lethargy and weakness
- Pale gums
- Diarrhoea
- Swollen belly

133

A fever is usually a sign that there is something more serious going on. Feel your dog's nose to see if it's wet or dry, and if it's much hotter than usual. Feel the temperature of his belly. If you have a thermometer, it will be useful to take his temperature through the ear. A normal temperature for a dog will be about 100 to 101 degrees fahrenheit. If it's above this, then your dog has a fever.

What does the vomit look like?

If you are able to, it can be very useful to take a sample of the vomit with you to the vet's. The colour and consistency of the vomit can be a sign of what is going on in your dog's stomach, so look closely.

If the vomit is yellow, it is usually just bile form the stomach and it could be that your dog has eaten something that just didn't agree with him. Mucus in the vomit is not a good sign and can mean there's an inflammation or even an ulcer. Blood in the vomit is also a serious problem to watch out for. If you're really not sure and you can't take a sample, you could try taking a picture on your phone for the vet to look at.

What causes vomiting in dogs?

A large number of illnesses and conditions can cause vomiting, so it's difficult to know anything before you've seen a vet.

Here are some of the more common causes of vomiting that the vet will need to rule out:
- Allergies
- Food intolerances - being fed treats from the table can often cause this
- Eating too much too fast
- Changes in diet
- Eating foreign objects - these can block the exit to the stomach
- Parasites such as worms
- Gastritis

- Inflammatory bowel disease
- Flipped or folded over stomach – common in deep chested breeds
- Tumour in the stomach or intestines
- Kidney and liver problems
- Heat stroke
- Pancreatitis
- Ear infections

How will the vet know what's causing the vomiting?

Generally the more information you can give your vet the easier it will be to make a diagnosis. A full physical examination will be given to start with. Then your vet might take a range of tests from bloods to urine analysis, and of course the vomit itself. He might also look at your dog's faeces. If he suspects there is a problem with the stomach itself, then the vet will want to look at it by doing an ultrasound or performing an endoscopy.

What is the treatment?

Because there are so many different causes of vomiting, treatment will really depend on what the underlying cause is. The vomiting itself can be tackled with anti-nausea drugs. To replenish any lost fluids your dog can be given fluids through an IV drip.

Other treatments might include:
- Antibiotics to treat any infections
- Pain relief if there is any swelling or inflammation
- Dietary changes, either permanent or temporary
- In some cases, you'll be advised to with hold food for 24 hours to give your dog's stomach a break and ease the vomiting. Then you can give some very bland, dry food and plenty of water.

List of common medicines

The following are some commonly prescribed medicines which your dog may be prescribed at some point in their life.

Advocate

What it does: Advocate is a parasiticide spot-on treatment given to dogs and cats for parasites. It offers broad protection both internally and externally against fleas, lice, heartworm, lungworm, gastrointestinal worms, mites and sarcoptic mange. It combines imidacloprid and moxidectin and has the ability to prevent, as well as treat, a large spectrum of parasites.

Possible forms: Commonly comes in a spot-in application that is applied to the skin between the shoulder blades. It often comes in packs of four with green being for small dogs, aqua being for medium size dogs, red being for larger dogs and blue for extra-large dogs.

Small dogs: 3-9 lbs. Medium dogs: 9.1 – 20 lbs. Large dogs: 20.1 – 55lbs. Extra-large dogs: 55.1 – 88lbs. Please weigh your dog beforehand for an accurate indication on which pack to use.

Dosage: Advocate provides protection for approximately four weeks, so it should be applied monthly.

Minimum dosage for cats is 10mg/kg body weight of imidacloprid, 1mg/kg body weight of moxidectin = 0.1 ml/kg body weight of Advocate.

- Small cats: 4kg or less: 0.4ml Advocate – 10mg minimum imidacloprid – 1mg minimum moxidectin
- Large cats: More than 4kg to 8kg: 0.8ml Advocate – 10-20mg imidacloprid – 1-2mg moxidectin

Minimum dosage for dogs is 10mg/kg body weight of imidacloprid, 2.5mg/kg body weight of moxidectin = 0.1 ml/kg body weight of Advocate. Small to medium dogs should have Advocate applied in one spot. Larger dogs may need three or four along the backbone.

- Dogs less than 4kg: 0.4ml Advocate – 10mg minimum imidacloprid – 2.5mg minimum moxidectin
- Dogs 4 – 10kg: 1ml Advocate – 10-25mg imidacloprid – 2.5-6.25mg moxidectin
- Dogs 10 – 25 kg: 2.5ml Advocate – 10-25mg imidacloprid – 2.5-6.25mg moxidectin
- Dogs 25 – 40kg: 4ml Advocate – 10-16mg imidacloprid – 2.5-4mg moxidectin

Precautions and side effects: Do not apply the application to damaged skin and, in larger dogs, avoid applying too much onto one area. Very few side effects have been reported, but do not apply more frequently than the instructions.

Cats and dogs should not ingest the treatment orally. Dogs six months old and over should be checked for parasites, such as heartworm, before being given the treatment. Do not use on puppies under 7 weeks old and kittens under 9 weeks old. Pets weighing less than 1kg or who are sick or have a medical condition must be assessed by a vet before treatment is considered.

Interactions with other drugs: Common medicines are not known to interact, but check with your vet if your cat or dog is taking any other treatments or medications. Do not use any other antiparasitic treatments with Advocate unless authorised by your vet.

Synulox

What it does: Synulox is one of the most well-known, and the most popular antibiotic for cats and dogs containing amoxicillin and clavulanic acid. It is used as an antibiotic to treat a large number of bacterial infections such as urinary tract infections, respiratory tract infections, gingivitis, abscesses, skin diseases and many more common problems.

Possible forms: Synulox is taken orally. Palatable tablets can be easy to give to cats and dogs as they contain a flavouring. The tablets can also be crushed and put into a small meal if necessary.

Dosage: Synulox tablets come in 50mg and 250mg. The advised dosage rate is 12.5mg/kg twice a day. Higher dosages can be given such as the doubling of the dosage to 25mg/kg for specific cases, but only a vet should make this decision.

50mg tablets dosage by body weight to be taken twice a day:
- 1-2kg – ½ tablet
- 3-5kg – 1 tablet
- 6-9kg - 2 tablets
- 10-13kg – 3 tablets
- 14-18kg – 4 tablets

250mg tablets dosage by body weight to be taken twice a day:
- 19-25kg – 1 tablet
- 26-35kg – 1 1/2 tablets
- 36-49kg – 2 tablets
- 50kg – 3 tablets

Within 5-7 days you will see an improvement after taking antiobiotics with most cases of infection or disease. Respiratory diseases can take between 8 and 10 days, chronic skin diseases between 10 and 20 days, and chronic cystitis between 10 and 28 days .

Precautions and side effects: Synulox should not be given to other smaller animals and extra care much be taken with smaller dogs and cats. Synulox belongs to be group of drugs that can sometimes cause hypersensitivity, so consult your vet immediately if an allergic reaction occurs. If your dog or cat shows signs of vomiting, diarrhoea or skin rashes you must tell your vet immediately.

Interactions with other drugs: Speak to your vet if your pet is taking bacteriostatic antibiotics such as tetracycline or erythromycin. Avoid mixing with aminoglycosides.

What it does: A non-steroidal anti-inflammatory drug otherwise known as NSAID and it contains robenacoxib. It can be used to treat pain and inflammation in cats and dogs, particularly musculoskeletal disorders for cats and chronic osteoarthritis for dogs.

Possible forms: Onsior is usually taken orally and the tablets are often palatable meaning your pet is more likely to want to eat them because of their flavouring.

Dosage: Onsior has been proven to be best taken without food or a minimum of half an hour after or before eating. Do not break the tablets. Response normally shows within 7 days, but if the condition shows no signs of improving, the drug should be stopped after 10 days. Long term administering of Onsior will require close monitoring from your vet. Advised dosage is 1mg/kg body weight to be taken once a day at the same time of day with a range of 1-2mg/kg.

Body weight and number of tablets by mg size for dogs:
- 2.5 - < 5kg - One 5mg tablet
- 5 - < 10kg – One 10mg tablet
- 10 - < 20kg – One 20mg tablet
- 20 - < 40kg – One 40mg tablet
- 40 – 80kg – Two 40mg tablets

Body weight and dosage amount of a typical 6mg tablet for cats:
- 2.5 - 6kg – One tablet
- 6.1 – 12kg – Two tablets

Precautions and side effects: Do not give Onsior with food. Do not give Onsior to dogs or cats with medical problems such as gastrointestinal ulceration. You must tell your vet about any other medical conditions before administering the medication.

Hypersensitivity can occur and should be reported to the vet if allergic reactions show. Tell your vet if the drug shows no signs of working after 10 days. Do not give to pregnant or lactating animals. Small cats and dogs or kittens and puppies under three months old may not be able to take this drug. Long term administering of Onsior requires close monitoring by your vet. Contact your vet if you notice vomiting, diarrhoea, weight loss or anorexia, poor appetite, lethargy or other abnormal symptoms.

Interactions with other drugs: Do not give Onsior with other NSAIDs or corticosteroids. Speak with your vet if your pet takes any other medication.

Indorex

What it does: Indorex is a flea spray used to kill off fleas and dust mites as well as prevent eggs and larvae from developing. It can be used around the household and is suitable for both dogs and cats. It contains permethrin, pyripoxyfen and piperonyl butoxide. It's also known to help allergies in both humans and pets.

Possible forms: Indorex only comes in a spray can and can be applied around the home. It should not used directly on animals or people.

Dosage: The spray comes in 500ml cans. Spray the areas and fabrics your dog or cat uses. Each can normally offers around 79 square metres of content. Shake well and hold the can approx. 50cm away from the item you are spraying. Avoid spraying for too long due to increased chances of inhalation. You can spray bedding, carpets, mats, skirting boards, tiles and so on. The 500ml can says it is effective for up to 12 months.

Precautions and side effects: Indorex is reportedly poisonous to insects, bees, fish and crustaceans. Use only in a cat or dog household. Do not apply the spray directly on your pet. Close the room and leave it for 30 minutes after spraying – once this is done you should ventilate the room for another 30 minutes, before allowing your pets or anyone back into the room. Avoid inhaling the spray. This is a product to use to accompany parasite treatment – it is not a substitute for it. Treat your dog or cat for fleas, other parasites and also use worming treatments – Indorex will then be more effective by preventing re-occurrence and killing off existing parasites. Avoid using around areas for food preparation. Do not spray near open flames. Vacuum before and after treatment and do this regularly. Humans and animals should not ingest Indorex, so tell your vet and your doctor if you or your pet is vomiting or has diarrhoea after your have treated your home with the spray.

Interactions with other drugs: Avoid using any other similar parasitic sprays. Speak to your vet before use if you have used a parasite treatment on your pet recently.

Robinul (Glycopyrrolate)

What it does: Robinul is also known as Glycopyrrolate and is a pre-anaesthetic anticholinergic used to decrease secretions in cats and dogs in the throat, mouth, airways and stomach which is normally given before operations. It can also be used during operations to stop unwanted reflexes and to prevent side effects from specific medications. It's known to be a contributing treatment for peptic ulcers and other medical conditions.

Possible forms: Most common form of Robinul is by injection. It also comes in tablet form. Which type used will be the decision of your vet

Dosage: The injections normally come in 0.2mg/ml concentrations in vials ranging from 1ml to 20ml. The drug is rarely given to pet owners to administer, so a vet will be responsible for dosage and giving glycopyrrolate.

- DOGS: 5 micrograms/lb body weight (0.25 mL per 10 lbs body weight)
- CATS: 5 micrograms/lb body weight (0.25 mL per 10 lbs body weight) Effect is best for cats when given 15 minutes before anaesthetics.

Precautions and side effects: The drug is normally safe when prescribed and handled by a veterinary professional. Some animals may show signs of hypersensivitiy (allergy). It should be used carefully if animal has a fast heart rate or suffers from a heart, liver or kidney condition. Some side effects can occur such as blurred vision, dry mouth, wobbly movement, drowsiness and excessive water consumption.

Interactions with other drugs: Glycopyrrolate may affect the performance of thiazide diuretics, nitrofurantoin, sympathomimetics and metoclopramide. Other interactions can be present when mixed with antihistamines, meperidine, diazepam and certain corticosteroids. Consult your vet before giving any medications to your cat or dog.

Vetmedin (Pimobendan)

What it does: Vetmedin is another name for pimobendan which is used to treat heart conditions for dogs. It treats congestive heart failure by opening up blood vessels from the heart and strengthening the heart beat in order for the heart to pump blood more effectively.

Possible forms: It is taken orally in capsules or flavoured tablets for easier administering to your dog.

Dosage: Vetmedin comes in 1.25 mg, 2.5 mg and 5 mg capsules. Dogs can be given 0.2 – 0.6 mg/kg body weight orally every 24 hours. This should be given one hour before meals. Improvements should begin within a week of taking the drug and is often a life-long medication.

Precautions and side effects: If your dog responds well to the drug it may be required to stay on it for life – in this case, regular check-ups with your vet are needed to monitor progress. Vetmedin is often taken well by dogs and side effects are rare, but could involve diarrhoea or vomiting. Tell your vet if you notice these symptoms.

Interactions with other drugs: Vetmedin is less effective when taken with beta-blockers or calcium-channel blockers. Digitalis glycosides are not known to interact. Contact your vet if your dog is taking other medications before taking Vetmedin.

Loxicom (Meloxicam)

What it does: Loxicom is another name for meloxicam or metacam, an NSAID for cats and dogs used to relieve pain and inflammation connected with surgery, osteoarthritis, injuries and many other causes associated with the musculoskeletal system.

Possible forms: Available as an injection or orally, depending on which method your vet prescribes.

Dosage:
- CATS: 0.3mg/kg subcutaneous, orally then 0.1 mg/kg orally every 24 hours for 4 days, then 1 drop/cat orally every 24 hours afterwards.
- DOGS: 0.2 mg/kg subcutaneous, orally just once for 1 day and then 0.1mg/kg orally every 24 hours afterwards.

Precautions and side effects: Must be avoided in cats and dogs with a hypersensitivity to its ingredients. Do not administer repeatedly as long-term effects can lead to renal failure or even death. Do not give more than instructed by your vet. Avoid giving to a pet with pre-existing renal problems. Avoid double dosing. Do not give this drug with any other NSAID unless instructed by a vet. Any cat or dog with a medical condition should not be given this drug unless your vet has given the ok – this also goes for pets already taking other medications. It is not suitable for use in pregnant pets. Diarrhoea or abnormal stools, seizures, inactivity, abnormal behaviour, jaundice, increased drinking and urination, skin irritations, stomach ulcers, vomiting or weight loss should be reported to a vet immediately.

Interactions with other drugs: NSAIDs and corticosteroids should not be used alongside this drug. Fluoroquinolones, anti-hypertensives/beta-blockers, diuretics and aminoglycosides should not be used alongside the drug unless otherwise stated by a vet.

Easeflex

What it does: Easeflex is a nutrional supplement that comes in various flavours and is made for both dogs and cats to relieve joint stiffness and increase mobility. It contains various ingredients, e.g. glucosamine, mucopolysaccharides, eicosatetraenoic acids, chondroitin, MSA, manganese, etc.

Possible forms: Easeflex is commonly given in tablet or chew form and normally won't need to be mixed or crushed into food. It can be given with or without food.

Dosage: Depends on the weight of the dog or cat and a trial of six weeks may be required beforehand. Speak to your vet about which specific amount you should give to your pet according to their individual needs.

- Under 5kg of weight – 1 chew a day
- Over 5kg of weight – 2 chews per day

Precautions and side effects: Easeflex is not to be used as a substitute for a healthy lifestyle. It should be used alongside regular exercise, a healthy monitored weight and a balanced diet. Speak to your vet if your dog has any medical conditions before giving Easeflex. Any vomiting, diarrhoea or similar reactions needs to be reported to a vet.

Reactions with other drugs: Easeflex often contains vitamin E, so avoid ingredients like this elsewhere to prevent too much vitamin E in the body. Consult your vet before giving this supplement if your pet already takes any kind of medication.

Marbocyl (Marbofloxacin)

What it does: Marbocyl is another name for marbofloxacin, a fluoroquinolone bactericidal agent used to tackle infections involving the respiratory system, skin, urinary tract, mammary glands and other areas.

Possible forms: Depends on the problem to be treated, but it can be taken orally, by injection or come in the form of a topical treatment. Oral marbocyl comes in 5 mg, 20 mg and 80 mg tablets. Injections come in 100 mg and 200 mg powders.

Dosage: Treatment duration varies on the problem, but can start from 5 days up to 30 days. Your vet will tell you how long.

DOGS AND CATS: 2mg/kg body weight daily in one dose, intravenous, subcutaneous or orally every 24 hours.

Precautions and side effects: Abnormal problems in the cartilage are known to be caused by similar fluoroquinlones, but less so in marbocyl. Side effects can include nausea, vomiting or diarrhoea. Caution must be taken with epileptic cats and dogs taking this drug. Do not exceed the recommended dosage as this could cause blindness as well as other health problems. Report any side effects to your vet. Also tell your vet of any medical conditions or medication already been taken beforehand.

Interactions with other drugs: Absorption may be problematical if marbocyl is taken with absorbents or antiacids that contain cations. Similar problems occur with sucralfate and zinc salts, so ask your vet for advice. Extra care must be taken if the pet has renal problems as they may be unable to take the drug. Taking cimetidine alongside marbocyl should be avoided.

Carprieve/Carprodyl/Carprofen

What it does: Carprieve is an NSAID analgesic medication given for inflammation, analgesia and pain relief for various problems, particularly arthritis and post-surgery pain. It is commonly used for dogs.

Possible forms: Normally tablets come flavoured to increase the chances of your dog taking it without any fuss. They come in three strengths: 20 mg, 50 mg and 100 mg.

Dosage: Given orally to dogs – first dose is 2 – 4 mg/kg body weight a day. Can be given as a single dose daily or can be divided into two dosages taken daily. After 7 days, the dosage is normally reduced to 2 mg/kg body weight a day as a single daily dose. Your vet will give you instructions. Duration varies depending on how your dog responds to the drug. If your dog is taking carprieve long-term they should be closely monitored by your vet. Specific dosages will be advised by your vet depending on the problem being treated.

Precautions and side effects: Carprieve is for dogs only. Use in cats is only the decision of a veterinary professional. Dogs suffering from medical conditions such as heart disease, hepatic disease, renal disease, gastric ulceration or similar conditions may not be able to use the drug. Avoid in dogs with a hypersensivity to the ingredients. Do not use with any other NSAIDs. Common side effects include vomiting, diarrhoea or softer faeces, bloody stools, poor appetite and lethargy – report these to a vet if witnessed. Avoid using in puppies under 4 months old. Extra care must be taken giving the drug to senior dogs. Avoid use in pregnant and lactating dogs. Reactions are severe if taken to excess.

Interactions with other drugs: Avoid the use of any other NSAID while taking carprieve. Consult your vet before giving the drug if your dog is already taking other medications. Avoid administering carpieve alongside anticoagulants.

Prednisolone

What it does: Prednisolone is a corticosteroid known as an anti-inflammatory, anti-fibrotic and immunosuppressive medication and is prescribed to manage inflammation, diseases and conditions particularly associated with the immune system, nervous system, cancer, skin, allergies, orthopaedic disease, hormones, respiratory disease, bowel disease and many other conditions of cats and dogs. It is a strong drug able to manage a broad spectrum of problems.

Possible forms: It can come in many forms and your vet will decide which form is best depending on the specific medical condition. Forms include eye drops, topical treatments, injections and oral medication.

Dosage for cats and dogs:
• Eye drops: Will depend on condition and best advised by vet (as are all medications), but generally 1 drop in the eye every 4 – 8

hours and this will reduce according to response.

- Allergy: Initially 0.5 – 1 mg/kg orally every 12 hours, reducing to the lowest every 48 hour dose.
- Anti-inflammatory: Cats – 1.1 mg/kg orally every 12 hours, reducing to 1.1 – 2.2 mg/kg every 48 hours. Dogs – 0.5 – 1 mg/kg orally every 12 hours, reducing to 0.5 – 1 mg/kg every 48 hours.
- Immunosuppression: Cats – 2.2 – 6.6 mg/kg orally every 12 hours, reducing to 2.2 – 4.4 mg/kg every 48 hours. Dogs – 1.1 – 3.3 mg/kg orally every 12 hours, reducing to 0.5 – 2.2 mg/kg every 48 hours.
- Hypoadrenocorticism: 0.2 – 0.3 mg/kg with fludrocortisone. Dosages are advised by the vet depending on the medical problem.

Precautions and side effects: Side effects are less likely in the short-term while taking prednisolone but more likely in the longer term. They include increased thirst and urination, increased appetite, greater risk of infections, fever, Cushing's disease, changes to coat, changes to abdominal shape and changes to behaviour such as aggression. Report any symptoms to your vet straight away. Avoid halting prednisolone suddenly and coming off or reducing the drug must be done gradually. As the drug affects the immune system your pet is more susceptible to infection, whether bacterial or viral. Double check with you vet if your pet is young, pregnant, lactating, taking other medicines or suffers from any medical problem.

Interactions with other drugs: Diabetic animals may need an alteration to their insulin intake when on prednisolone. Tell your vet if your pet is on any other medications. Aspirin, salicylates, mitotane, erythromycin, cyclosporine, phenytoin, phenobarbital, rifampin, diuretic, amphotericin B, furosemide, pyridostigmine, neostigmine, other anticholinesterase medications, etc. Ulcers can occur if taken with other NSAIDs. Your vet will need to monitor your pet's progress while on the drug.

Zylkene

What it does: Zylkene is a natural, stress management medication that helps dogs and cats deal with changes and other stressful situations.

These can include having to stay somewhere other than home, going to a new home, dealing with new residents or animals, loud noises such as fireworks, travelling, visiting the vet, big social events held at home, etc.

Possible forms: Zylkene is given in capsules, but these are not be swallowed whole. You open the capsule yourself and sprinkle the contents into the cat or dog's food. It is normally palatable, so it is less likely to put your pet off their food compared to other, non-natural medications. They come in 75 mg capsules for small dogs and cats, 225 mg for medium dogs and 450 mg for large dogs.

Dosage: Give once a day for as long as instructed by your vet.

- Cats and small dogs under 10kg – One 75 mg capsule a day.
- Medium dogs between 10 – 20kg – One 225 mg capsule a day.
- Large dogs between 20 – 40kg – One 450 mg capsule a day.

People with dogs over 40kg need to consult their vet on dosage, which is typically double the dose per day.

Precautions and side effects: If behavioural problems continue to persist even after treatment you should tell your vet. Tell your vet of any medical conditions or medications taken before zylkene is given. Side effects are not commonly associated with the product, but tell your vet immediately if you notice anything unusual. It is hypoallergenic and does not contain ingredients likely to cause irritation such as preservatives or lactose. Your vet may want to re-assess your pet's stress levels after a few weeks.

Interactions with other drugs: Zylkene is often safe to use with other products, but consult your vet first to be sure.

Fortekor (Benazepril)

What it does: Fortekor is another name for benazepril, its prime ingredient. It is a drug used for both cats and dogs to treat heart failure and chronic renal insufficiency. It is known for increasing the quality of life and the lifespan of cats and dogs.

Possible forms: Fortekor is taken orally and the tablet is often flavoured to make it more palatable. The tablets come in 5 mg and 20 mg.

Dosage:
- Cats with chronic renal insufficiency: 0.5 – 1 mg/kg orally every 24 hours.
- Dogs with heart failure: 0.25 – 0.5 mg/kg orally every 24 hours.

Precautions and side effects: Side effects may include hyperkalaemia, hypotension (tiredness, weakness, dizziness) or renal impairment. If any unusual signs are seen you must tell your vet immediately. Fortekor is not suitable for pregnant or lactating dogs or cats and breeding dogs or cats. Progress must be monitored regularly by your vet.

Interaction with other drugs: Specific drugs may trigger reactions, so it's important to check with your vet that fortekor is safe to use alongside any other drugs. Potassium preserving medications or diuretics such as spironolactone or potassium supplementation could cause unnecessary side effects. Avoid using NSAIDs alongside fortekor unless it is cleared with your vet. Other anti-hypertensives given alongside fortekor can also cause side effects. Consult your vet if your cat or dog takes any of the above.

Cerenia

What it does: Cerenia is used to help prevent nausea in dogs, whether it's from sickness brought on by chemotherapy, motion sickness, and vomiting from other causes.

Possible forms: The most common forms of cerenia are injection and tablet. Injection is normally administered within a veterinary clinic or hospital whilst the tablet can be given at home. Tablets commonly come in 16 mg, 24 mg, 60 mg and 160 mg strengths.

Dosage: Ensure your dog has not eaten at least one hour before giving the dose. Give cerenia 2 hours before travelling.

- Preventing acute vomiting: 0.9 mg/lb body weight orally once a day. Dosage for up to 5 days.
- Preventing motion sickness vomiting: 3.6 mg/lb body weight orally once a day. Done for up to 2 days.

Precautions and side effects: Using cerenia to treat acute vomiting is only recommended for dogs aged 8 weeks and older. Using it for motion sickness is only recommended for dogs aged 16 weeks and older. Avoid giving the drug in your dog's food and try not to fast your dog for prolonged periods beforehand – an hour is sufficient.

Side effects may include drowsiness, tiredness, drooling, diarrhoea and, in severe cases, anorexia. Tell your vet immediately if you notice any of these signs. Avoid using this medication if your dog is allergic to maropitant citrate. Avoid use in breeding dogs, pregnant dogs and lactating dogs.

If your dog suffers from epilepsy, seizures, heart disease, kidney disease or any other medical condition it needs to be addressed and extra care must be taken before being prescribed cerenia. Bloody faeces, poor appetite, bad diarrhoea or lack of activity should be reported to your vet immediately as this could be a sign of a bad reaction or an overdose.

Interactions with other drugs: Your regular vet will know what other medications your dog is taking and, if safe to use, cerenia will be prescribed by your vet. To be certain always check with your vet beforehand if you give your dog any kind of treatment.

Torbugesic (Butorphanol)

What it does: Torbugesic, also known as butorphanol or torbutrol, is a form of pain relief and a cough suppressant that is used in various animals, particularly cats and dogs. Additionally, it has proved to be effective in preventing vomiting in pets going through chemotherapy.

Common forms: Torbugesic can be given by injection or orally as tablets. Injections are typically 10 mg/ml solutions and the tablets come in 5 mg and 10 mg strengths.

Dosage:
- Cats: 0.05 – 0.6 mg/kg intramuscular, subcutaneous as required, otherwise every 6 – 8 hours.
- Dogs – antitussive: 0.05 – 0.1 mg/kg intramuscular, subcutaneous or 0.5 – 1 mg/kg orally every 6 – 12 hours.
- Dogs – analgesic: 0.05 – 0.6 mg/kg intravenous, intramusclar, subcutaneous as required, otherwise every 6 – 8 hours.
- Dogs – anti-emetic before chemotherapy: 0.2 – 0.6 mg/kg subcutaneous.

Precautions and side effects: Side effects can involve diarrhoea, anorexia, sedation or affected coordination, but this is often quite rare. Pets with Addisons' disease, increased CSF pressure, hypothyroidism or renal insufficiency should be dealt cautiously with torbugesic. Avoid use of torbugesic in pets with pancreatitis. Extra care must be taken with pets with hepatic or renal function problems. Talk to your vet in the event of side effects, other medications or medical conditions.

Interactions with other drugs: Torbugesic can affect animals also taking tranquillizers, barbiturates, phenothiazines and other CNS depressants. Also, avoid use with metoclopramide and pancuronium unless cleared by a vet.

Aurizon

What it does: Aurizon is a brand of ear drops made for dogs to treat fungal and bacterial otitis externa – this condition involves inflammation and redness of the external ear canal. It contains marbofloxacin, dexamethasone and clotrimazole.

Possible forms: Aurizon comes in the form of ears drops and would usually require a prescription from your vet.

Dosage: Shake the Aurizon before use. Apply 10 drops into your dog's ear once a day for 7 to 14 days depending on the instructions from your vet. Normally after a week your vet will want to examine the ear to determine whether you should continue the treatment or not. Clean the area before applying the drops, apply the drops and then massage the ear base to encourage the drops to reach the affected canal.

Precautions and side effects: There is a risk of contamination if you are treating more than one dog with the same Aurizon application. Use a different cannula on each dog. Do not give the drops to pregnant or lactating dogs. Avoid use in dogs sensitive to the ingredients. Avoid use in dogs with perforation of the tympanic membrane. Do not use the product for prolonged periods. If you notice your dog has a loss of hearing or any other unusual problems while taking these drops you should contact your vet as soon as possible.

Interactions with other drugs: Avoid using any other ear drops or medications with the same ingredients. If your dog has a medical condition or is taking any other medication you must tell your vet before treatment starts.

Vivitonin (Propentofylline)

What it does: Vivitonin is a medication used to help lethargic, dull dogs who need improvements to their demeanour. It is used commonly in older dogs and improves their well-being by increasing their energy and enthusiasm to exercise. It does this by improving and increasing blood flow to the heart, central nervous system, muscles and brain.

Possible forms: Oral tablets with strengths ranging from 50 mg to 100 mg.

Dosage: For dogs only – 2.5 – 5 mg/kg orally every 12 hours. Give the medication 30 minutes prior to meals.

Precautions and side effects: Avoid use in pregnant and lactating dogs. Avoid use in dogs with medical conditions such as kidney disease – check with your vet. Avoid in dogs hypersensitive to the drug. Rare side effects include vomiting or allergic reactions, which must be reported to your vet if noticed. Dosage should be reduced in dogs with renal problems.

Interactions with other drugs: Dogs already taking medication for congestive heart failure or bronchial disease should not be given vivitonin.
Speak to your vet about any medications being taken.

Buprecare/Buprenorphine/Vetergesic

What it does: Vetergesic is otherwise known as buprecare or buprenorphine. It is an analgesic used to control pain in cats and dogs, but can
be given to other animals too.

Possible forms: Buprenorphine is given as an injection – 0.3 mg/ml
solution.

Dosage: For cats and dogs – 0.006 – 0.02 mg/kg intravenous, intramuscular, subcutaneous every 8 hours or as required.

Precautions and side effects: In some cases severe pain may not go away
with buprenorphine and increasing intake can be ineffective and
is not recommended, so vets often advise the use of an alternative
medication. Avoid using buprenorphine in animals with pancreatitis.
Extra care must be taken in animals with liver problems. Avoid use
in pregnant and lactating animals. Take care giving to animals with
respiratory problems. Avoid use in pets younger than 7 weeks old.
Avoid prolonged use. Report any unusual symptoms or behaviour to
your vet straight away.

Interactions with other drugs: Avoid use if pet is taking morphine, pethi-
dine or similar treatments unless advised by a vet. Your vet should be
aware of other medications already being taken by your pet before
buprenorphine is prescribed.

Urilin

What it does: Urilin treats dogs with urinary incontinence caused by
urethral sphincter incompetence. This problem is common in spayed
bitches. It contains phenylpropanolamine, which is effective in stimu-

153

lation of sphincter muscles.

Possible forms: Urilin comes in a syrup taken orally.

Dosage: 0.8 mg/kg body weight phenylpropanolamine 3 times a day in the feed, corresponding to 0.1 ml urilin syrup /5 kg body weight 3 times a day. 1 drop per 2.34 kg weight 3 times a day with feed.

Precautions and side effects: Pets treated with monoamine oxidase inhibitors should not use this medicine. Do not use this medicine to attempt to solve urination caused by behavioural problems. The medicine contains ingredients that affect the heart rate and blood pressure of your pet, so be cautious if your pet has heart problems or low/high blood pressure. Take care using the medicine with pets suffering from hepatic or renal insufficiency, diabetes, glaucoma, hyperadrenocorticism and other similar metabolic disorders. Signs of poisoning can occur if overdosed and can be fatal – signs include headache, nausea, dizziness, high blood pressure and insomnia. Keep this medicine stored safely and securely. Softer faeces, diarrhoea, poor appetite, arrhythmia or any other unusual side effects should be reported to a vet immediately. Avoid use in pregnant or lactating dogs.

Interactions with other drugs: Be careful giving urilin with other sympathomimetic medications, anticholinergic medications, tricyclic antidepressants or type B monoamine oxidase. Consult your vet if your dog already takes medication.

Soloxine (Levothyroxine/L-Thyroxine)

What it does: Soloxine is another name for levothyroxine and it treats hypothyroidism in both cats and dogs as well as other animals. If your pet's thyroid isn't working as it should, soloxine can be the thyroid replacement it needs and helps the typical symptoms of hyperthyroidism such as poor energy and gain in weight. This is seen particularlyin older animals.

Possible forms: Soloxine is given in tablet form and it comes in various strengths: 0.1 mg, 0.2 mg, 0.3 mg, 0.5 mg and 0.8 mg.

Dosage: 0.02 – 0.04 mg/kg/day. Or alternative dosage is 0.5 mg/m2 body surface area every day. Dosage is given once a day or split into twice a day depending on the animal's response or request of the vet.

Precautions and side effects: Caution needs to be taken with pets suffering from cardiac disorders or adrenal insufficiency. Signs of overdose include overexcited behaviour, nervous behaviour, increased panting and tachycardia. Any unusual signs need to be addressed by a vet quickly. If your pet suffers from any medical condition it is best to consult your vet before this medication is given.

Interactions with other drugs: Soloxine may interact with various medications, so it is important to consult with your vet about anything you already give your pet. Examples of drugs that can interact include epinephrine, norepinephrine, estrogens, insulin, warfarin, digoxin, vitamins, supplements and many others.

Milbemax (Milbemycin)

What it does: Milbemax, otherwise known as milbemycin, is a worming medication that treats a cat or dog infected with cestodes and nematodes, which are types of parasitic worm.

Possible forms: It is given orally and the tablets come in strengths of 2.3 mg, 5.75mg, 11.5 mg, 23 mg including lufenuron for program plus, 2.5 mg, 4 mg, 12.5 mg tablets including praziquantel for milbemax.

Dosage:
- Cats – Milbemax 2 mg/kg orally once.
- Dogs – 0.5 mg/kg orally once.

Milbemax should be given with food or after meals. Ask your vet for advice on medication before the start and after the mosquito season, regarding heartworm prevention. This usually involves medicating one month before and one month after this period.

Precautions and side effects: Some dogs may be affected with paler skin, eyelids, insides of the mouth and other mucous membranes. Some may suffer slight diarrhoea as the movement of waste through the intestines is increased while taking Milbemax. Signs of overdose include poor co-ordination, fever an increased need to lie down or sit periodically. Discuss any medical conditions with your vet before the drug is given. Report any side effects to your vet.

Interactions with other drugs: Take care using milbemax with other macrocyclic lactones. Other interactions are not known, but your vet will see any medications your pet is taking and will verify whether taking milbemax is safe to do so with others.

Fuciderm Gel

What it does: Fuciderm gel is an aqueous treatment with the ingredients of fusidic acid, betamethasone and methylparahydroxybenzoate, and propylparahydroxybenzoate. It's topical and treats dogs with moist dermatitis and intertrigo, which is a type of skin fold dermatitis. It has anti-inflammatory and antibiotic qualities.

Possible forms: It is an aqueous, topical treatment gel that comes in a tube.

Dosage: For dogs only – Apply a thin amount to the affected area twice a day for approximately 5 days depending on your vet's instructions. Treatment is normally advised to continue for a further two days when the lesion has gone. Avoid exceeding 7 days.

Precautions and side effects: It is best administered while wearing gloves. If the gel shows no sign of working after 3 days consult your vet. Do not use for prolonged periods. If your dog reacts badly to the gel, stop use immediately and consult your vet.

Avoid use in hypersensitive dogs. Deep pyoderma requires other treatments. Avoid use in areas where fungal infection is present. Do not use on or near the dog's eyes. Prevent your dog from licking the affected area and the gel - a collar may be needed. Avoid treating large areas. Report any unusual side effects to your vet quickly. Do not use on lactating or pregnant dogs.

Interactions with other drugs: Do not use with other similar topical treatments unless stated otherwise by your vet. Other interactions are not known.

Gabapentin

What it does: Gabapentin can be given to both cats and dogs and it helps as an analgesic to relieve pain and it also works as an anti-convulsant for certain cases of epilepsy and seizures. It commonly treats dysfunctional or damaged nerves and pain caused by cancers.

Possible forms: Gabapentin is given orally and comes in tablet dosages of 100 mg, 300 mg, 400 mg and 600 mg.

Dosage: Dosage depends on which problem is being treated and will be advised by your vet. Duration and strength of dosage will depend on the circumstances and how your cat or dog responds to the drug.

Examples and rough approximations:
- Pain in dogs and cats: 1.4 mg/lb once a day.
- Seizures in dogs: 4.5 – 13.5 mg/lb body weight every 12 hours.
- Seizures in cats: 2.3 mg/lb 3 times a day.

Precautions and side effects: Side effects could include vomiting, diarrhea, imbalance or drowsiness. Report any signs to your vet. Avoid in animals allergic to gabapentin. Do not use the drug in pregnant or lactating animals. Take care giving the drug to animals with kidney disease. Consult with your vet before giving gabapentin to a pet with a medical condition. Coming off gabapentin should be done gradually, never stop immediately, your vet can advise the safest reductions.

Interactions with other drugs: Do not give your pet gabapentin containing xylitol. Avoid the use of antacids, morphine and hydrocodone. Speak to your vet if your animal is already taking other medications.

Yumove

What it does: Yumove is a supplement that helps keep the joints of cats and dogs healthy by providing the vital nutrients needed. It is also beneficial for pets who already have joint problems and arthritis, so it is not only a preventative method but a form of management and treatment, too. These supplements are normally flavoured to make consumption easier, and contain natural ingredients including the beneficial glucosamine and chondroitin. Some also contain vitamins.

Possible forms: Yumove is often taken orally in the form of a capsule or tablet, and can be supplied in batches of 60, 120 and 300. These are often flavoured so are very palatable.

Dosage: Tablets are branded for cats and dogs, so each should provide the recommended amount in the individual tablet. It's advised to start the dose and reduce it after a few weeks:

Dogs:
- 15kg weight or less – 2 tablets a day
- 16 – 30 kg – 4 tablets a day
- 31 – 45 kg – 6 tablets a day
- Over 45kg – 8 tablets a day

After two weeks it is recommended to half these initial dosages.

Cats:
4 - 5 kg - 1 a day

Ask your vet about specific dosages, initial dosages and when to half the dosage.

Precautions and side effects: Ensure to half the dosage after the initial period. Take care in cats or dogs with medical conditions and ensure the supplement is cleared to use by your vet. If you notice any vomiting, diarrhoea or other side effects consult your vet.

Interactions with other drugs: As Yumove sometimes includes vitamins and other supplements, you should avoid giving them other supplements and vitamins of the same type, this will ensure their body doesn't have too much of any one vitamin, which can be bad for their health!

Tell your vet if your cat or dog takes any other drugs.

Destolit (Ursodeoxycholic acid)

What it does: Destolit, also known as ursodeoxycholic acid, affects the biliary system of a dog or cat. It is used to help animals with cholestatic liver disease.

Possible forms: Destolit is taken orally and comes in various strengths including 150 mg, 300 mg tablets, 250 mg capsules and 50 mg/ml suspension.

Dosage: For both cats and dogs: 10 – 15 mg/kg orally every 24 hours.

Precautions and side effects: Side effects are rare, but can involve vomiting, and you should consult your vet if this occurs. Any other unusual signs should also be reported. Take care in pets with medical conditions. Your vet will tell you of any precautions if applicable. Your vet will need to closely monitor your cat or dog's progress.

Interactions with other drugs: Tell your vet of any medication or supplementation you are giving your pet before using Destolit.

Behaviour

Understanding your dog:

Anthropomorphism

Anthropomorphism refers to the practice of attributing human characteristics to something other than a human, such as an object or animal. A common example of anthropomorphism is the Dog owner who treats her canine pet as a human member of the family. This behaviour typically means that the dog is showered with an abundance of love and affection which, of course, is a wonderful thing. The bond we have with our pets can become very strong if we imagine that they are experiencing feelings and emotions similar to our own. However, anthropomorphism can also be a destructive force when trying to establish healthy relationships between Dogs and their owners.

In general, dogs tend to thrive when they are given rules and limitations. Setting clear boundaries for your Dog's behaviour is essential in enabling you to live together in a safe and harmonious way. Reminding yourself of the fact that your dog isn't a human (no matter how much he may act like one) will help you to understand why he behaves the way he does, and the steps you can take to modify his behaviour if necessary.

Language and relationships

Language is one of the most effective tools for developing a healthy relationship with your Dog. Examples of the ways that you can use language to communicate with your dog include:

A strong tone of voice to assert your dominance and discipline. This is important to let your dog know that you make the rules and when his behaviour is unacceptable.

Key command words to train your dog to behave in a particular way. "Sit" and "stay" are common examples of these command words. Kind and affectionate language should be used to reward good behaviour and to demonstrate your love and happiness with your dog. A reassuring and comforting tone may be necessary if your dog is timid or scared.

Body language

Unfortunately, your Dog is unable to use words to communicate how she is feeling to you. Instead of words, there are some key body language signals that you can look for as a guide to understanding your dog's emotions and behaviour. These include:

His tail

Action	What It May Mean
Wagging Low	Joy and Contentment
Wagging High	Playfulness

Held Stiff	Hostility
Tucked between the legs	Fear

His ears

Action	What It May Mean
Pricked and head tilted to the side	Curiousity
Laid Back Against The Head	Fear or Aggression

His mouth

Action	What It May Mean
Slow pant	Happy and Relaxed
Fast Pant	Tired, hot or stressed
Lips Pulled Back Revealing Teeth and Gums	Aggression

His body

Action	What It May Mean
Bowing down with tail wagging	Playfulness
Staying Low To The Ground Clutching	Possessiveness
Standing Tall	Confidence and Pride
Stretching	Tiredness or relaxation
Rolling over to expose the belly	Comfortable and wanting affection
Fur standing upright	Fear or Aggression
Pacing back and forth, or shaking	Stress or Fear
Circling or mounting another dog	Dominance

Trust and respect

As with any healthy relationship, it is vital that a dog and its owner trust and respect each other. Your Dog needs to trust that you will

162

take care of his basic needs, not mistreat him, and give him the comfort and security he needs to live a healthy and happy life. You need to be able to trust that he is not going to harm you or other people or animals. You also need to be able to trust that he will behave appropriately around your possessions and in public places. A big part of trusting your dog means being confident that he will obey your commands.

Whether your Dog chooses to obey you or not will depend upon whether he respects you as the dominant leader. Being clear and consistent with training, discipline and rewards will encourage him to respect your authority.

It is also important that you maintain a healthy level of respect for your dog. Keep in mind that some of your dog's behaviour is governed by animal instinct and that many of the situations he encounters in a domestic environment may be confusing or intimidating for him. This may cause him to behave in an unpredictable or undesirable way.

Once mutual trust and respect has been established between you and your Dog, the loyalty and unconditional love will flourish and you will develop an unbreakable bond.

Kindness, empathy and guidance

It goes without saying that all pets should be treated with kindness. It is arguable that kindness is particularly important for Dogs because of their loyal and companionable nature. Many Dogs demonstrate an unquenchable desire to please their owners. Rewarding their good behaviour with praise and love is vitally important for their health and well-being.

Empathy is also an important emotion to show towards your canine companion. Recognise that certain occasions may make him feel scared, insecure and uncertain. An urban environment can be a bewildering place for an animal and your dog will turn to you for guidance support in trying to understanding the world. Making an effort to empathise with him can help you to appreciate why he is behaving in a certain way and what you can do to help.

Survival instinct

Another essential factor in understanding your dog's behaviour is accepting that some of his actions occur due to an innate survival instinct. As with other animals, dogs have evolved in accordance with the "survival of the fittest" principle.

This manifests in modern domesticated dogs in a variety of ways. Possessiveness or aggression around their food, territorial behaviour in their home and barking when being approached by a stranger are actions that would have helped a wild dog to survive.

When Dogs behave according to these instincts in a domestic environment it can be frustrating and potentially dangerous. Utilising the training techniques outlined later in this book can help you to improve your dog's behaviour.

Behavioural cycle

If you own a female Dog then you will need to be aware of her ovulation cycle, as this can have a big impact on her attitude and behaviour. When females are in heat the hormone changes can cause her to become agitated and aggressive. This happens twice a year, for around three weeks at each time. Having your dog spayed can help to reduce or even eliminate these behavioural problems.

Feeding

Good feeding habits

As with all other training and discipline issues, the key to building and maintaining good feeding habits in your Dog is consistency. Establishing a set feeding routine will help him to learn that he can rely upon you, and that he needs to behave in an acceptable manner.

Consistency in feeding your Dog means:
- having regular mealtimes
- always feeding him in the same location
- giving him a food bowl and water bowl that he can recognise as "his"
- making sure that he isn't interrupted while eating
- not feeding him scraps of food in the kitchen while you're cooking, or at the table while you're eating.

Consistency does not refer to the type of food that you feed your Dog. As with humans, most dogs enjoy variety and will benefit from a diverse and nutritious meal-plan.

Priority feeding

Priority feeding is a training technique that is designed to teach your Dog that you are in control of the food, and that he needs to respect you and your rules in order to receive it.

It is based on the humans and the dog having separate meals, and the humans of the household having priority in the food receiving hierarchy.

It is recommended that you implement the following step-by-step process for two to three weeks with a new dog in order to establish good feeding habits:

1. Prepare your dog's meal and some food for yourself.
2. Eat a small amount of your food in your dog's view and then put his food bowl down on the ground. Don't say anything or make eye contact.
3. Walk away from the dog food, but stay nearby. If you leave the room then the dog may leave his meal and follow you.
4. If your dog walks away from the food bowl, then pick it up, whether the food has been eaten or not.

5. Ensure that your dog always has access to fresh, clean water.

Once your Dog has learned that you control the food, and that he can trust you to feed him sufficiently, then you can stop the priority feeding system. You can always re-introduce this method again at a later date should he need reminding about good food manners.

Staying in control

If you don't want your canine companion to beg at the table when you are eating, or to steal food from the kitchen, then you need to stay in control of the food situation in your household. Relenting to your Dog's begging, and feeding him from your meals, will send him a clear message that this behaviour is acceptable. This can then become a very difficult habit to break.

If your dog is persistently begging for food then you may need to take further steps to discourage this behaviour. Restricting access to these areas of the house at certain times is one effective step. It may also help to give him something else to occupy his time while the humans are eating, such as his own meal, a bone, or a chew-toy.

It's also important that you stay in control of the use of treats. Treats should only ever be used as a reward for your Dog when they have obeyed a command or done something else that pleases you. Giving a dog treats for no reason at all reduces their effectiveness as a training aid and reward.

Food aggression

Some Dogs can be very aggressive around food. It may be that they have experienced difficult conditions in the past in which they needed to fight for survival. Whatever the reason, food aggression can present a very dangerous situation for people or other animals that happen to be around the little dog while he is feeding. If your dog displays aggressive behaviour around his food, it is important that you take action to reduce this danger and to make your home safer.

First, let's start with what NOT to do. If your Dog is aggressive around food then don't leave food out for him at all times. He should only be fed at scheduled meal times and then once he's finished eating his bowl should be taken away, even if it still has food in it. Leaving it out can be confusing and unsettling for him as he thinks he needs to protect it all the time. Don't yell at or punish your Dog for food guarding. He is exhibiting a natural competitive instinct and you have to work with him to overcome it. Trying to dominate and overpower him may work against you as it could encourage him to become more aggressive. It may also cause him to distrust or fear you which can damage your relationship.

Carefully consider the safety of yourself, your family and any other people or animals when your Dog is feeding. If he needs to be restrained on a leash, or isolated from others while eating, then this should be done until you feel confident that he can be trusted not to snap and bite. When it comes to overcoming your dog's food aggression, your primary purpose is to make him relax and feel comfortable when people approach him while he's eating.

Changing this attitude is a very gradual process that may take some weeks to complete. You should take it at a pace that you and your dog are comfortable with. Trying to rush through this process is counter-productive as it may result in your dog becoming stressed which will then trigger the aggression.

The method outlined below is based on convincing your Dog that when someone approaches his bowl they may be bringing something much better and more exciting than what he's currently eating. This will help him establish positive connotations for people approaching him and will hopefully eradicate his fear and aggression.

Step 1
Put a bowl of dry kibble on the floor for your dog. Once he begins eating, stand a comfortable distance back from him and don't approach any closer. Talk to him in a calm, conversational tone and regularly toss a small treat towards him. The treat can be anything

your Dog really enjoys, such as beef, chicken, cheese or sausage.

He will probably turn his attention away from the bowl to get the treats. If he comes towards you for more treats, just ignore him and only start throwing them again once he returns to his bowl. Continue this method for a week or so, or until he seems at ease with this.

Step 2

Take all the same actions as in step 1 above, only this time move a step towards your Dog each time you toss him the treat. After throwing the treat, step back to your starting position. Each day, begin a little bit closer to his bowl. Continue this for a week or so, until he is comfortable with you standing around two feet away from him while he's eating.

Step 3

Put the bowl of dry kibble down for your Dog and walk away. Once he starts eating, approach him using the same conversational tone and words that you have been using in the previous steps.

When you are standing right next to your dog's bowl, drop a treat into it and then walk away. Repeat this regularly until he finishes his meal. Do this for around two weeks or until your dog is completely comfortable with you approaching him while he's at his bowl.

Step 4

Put the dry kibble down as in previous steps. Approach your dog using the same language as before. When you're beside him, hold the treat out in your hand and bend down toward him. Tempt him to stop eating from the bowl and to take the treat from your hand. Repeat this process until he finishes eating. Continue this step for a week or two, getting closer to your dog each time.

Step 5

Continue the same actions as in step 5, except this time touch your Dog's bowl with one hand while you're offering him the treat with the other hand.

168

Step 6

Begin as in step 5, but this time you want to pick the bowl up off the ground, drop the treat into it, and then return the bowl to the ground. Start by only picking the bowl up a few inches off the ground, and then gradually increase the height until you are lifting it to your waist. As you and your dog become more confident and comfortable with this routine, you can then begin to take the bowl to a nearby table or counter to put the treat in it before returning it to the usual spot on the floor. The point of this exercise is for the dog to understand that if you take the bowl off him while he's eating, it will be returned to him with something better and more exciting in it.

The 6 steps outlined above are designed to give your dog positive mental associations with you approaching him when he's eating. This will help to ease or eradicate his food aggression. You will need to repeat this process with each member of your family feeding your Dog to enable him to feel comfortable eating in front of everyone in the household.

Barking

There are many different reasons why a Dog barks. It may be due to excitement, boredom, fear, loneliness, guarding its territory, or raising an alarm when something unusual is going on. Sometimes you may appreciate your little dog barking. If you want to be alerted when people are visiting your property. However, at many other times a Dog's incessant barking can become an extreme annoyance for its owners and other people in the neighbourhood.

Identifying why he is barking is the first step in controlling this disruptive behaviour. You may find that you are able to identify different types of barks – for instance, his "I'm excited and I want to play" bark will probably sound quite different to his territorial or warning bark. If you know what's causing the bark, then you can be more focused on trying to reduce it. It's unrealistic to expect a dog to stop barking altogether; this is one of their primary means of communication. However, there are some steps that you can take to reduce your dog's barking in certain situations.

Barking in the house may be territorial or attention-seeking. He may also get very excited when people come to visit and barking is his way of greeting them. Whatever the reason, barking in the home can be annoying and off-putting for visitors, particularly if the dog is difficult to control.

If your Dog is barking to get attention or a reward from you, such as play, a walk, a toy or food, then you need to take firm steps to show him that this behaviour is unacceptable. If you give him what he wants in response to his barking, then the lesson he learns is that barking is the best way for him to communicate and he will do it more and more often.

Barking in the garden

Your Dog may be barking in the garden because he is territorial, bored, excited, communicating with other dogs in the neighbour-hood, or trying to get your attention.

Making sure that he has toys to play with, that he has a comfortable place to rest, and that he gets a lot of exercise and affection from you may help to reduce his barking outside. A large bone, or a chew-toy that he has to work at to release treats, can also help to distract him from barking for long periods of time. If your dog is barking in the garden while you're at home, then bring him into the house and only let him outside when he has stopped barking.

Repeat this behaviour whenever he barks. If he is jumping up at a window while inside and continuing to bark, then use a leash to se-cure him to a table or chair so that he can't see outside.

Barking on a walk

A dog barking on a walk could be an indication of excitement or alarm. If there is a trigger for his barking, such as when he is approached by a person, another dog, a bike or a car, then you can try to distract him during these moments to prevent the bark.

Hold a treat in front of his nose and allow him to nibble at it while the thing that he would normally bark at is passing by. Praise him if he doesn't bark.

Dealing with excessive barking

The first step in dealing with excessive barking is to identify why your Dog is barking in the first place.

Dog is barking in the first place. Think about when and where the barking occurs. What seems to trigger the barking? Does it only happen at a certain time of day or in a specific location? Once you understand the cause of the barking, then you can take steps to reduce it. In some instances, the easiest cause of action in reducing your dog's barking will be to remove the triggers.

If the dog can't see the things that are making him bark, then the barking will probably reduce. This may mean installing a fence that he can't see through, and restricting his access to the front door so he won't know when visitors are arriving.

Another way of dealing with excessive barking is to train your canine companion to be quiet on command. This requires a lot of dedication and patience, but it is well worth it as it will allow you to deal with all types of barking in a range of different locations and scenarios. This training method uses the reward system to teach your dog the meaning of the word "quiet" and to give you more control over his barking.

When a barking trigger occurs (for example, a visitor arrives at your house), allow your dog to bark a couple of times and then say "quiet" calmly and confidently. Don't shout it as that will just suggest to your dog that loud noises are acceptable. Hold him by the collar with one hand and gently hold his mouth closed with your other hand and repeat "quiet". Once he has calmed down, let him go and ask him to sit beside you. Then reward him with a special treat. Encourage him to sit quietly beside you for a few minutes or until the trigger has passed by repeating "quiet" and frequently giving him more treats. Over time, he should learn that being quiet on command pleases you and gets him rewards.

Aggression

The potential for aggression is a very important factor when you are considering bringing a Dog into your home to live with you and your family. Dogs have sharp teeth and claws which can cause serious harm to people and other animals if they choose to attack. Dealing with any dog attack is a terrifying and devastating experience for all involved, and all possible steps should be taken to stop these horrible situations from occurring.

At the end of the day, you are responsible for your Dog's behaviour. If he attacks someone, then you may face severe consequences. In some locations, dogs who act aggressively and who harm people or other animals, are required to be put down. This is why it's so important that you do all that you can to ensure that your four-legged friend isn't aggressive. Some of the risk factors associated with aggression include:

History

If you're adopting a Dog from an animal shelter, then the shelter owners should be able to give you a good idea of the dog's history and temperament. Find out whether he ended up at the shelter due to behavioural issues, and ask what his temperament has been like at the shelter. Dogs have sharp teeth and claws which can cause serious harm to people and other animals if they choose to attack. Dealing with any dog attack is a terrifying and devastating experience for all involved, and all possible steps should be taken to stop these horrible situations from occurring.

A dog may display some minor aggressive behaviour, for example, growling or showing his teeth, as a warning signal only and will not go any further. These less severe displays may make the dog easier to live with than dogs whose aggression is more severe. Of course, it can be very difficult to trust that the aggression will not get more severe in certain circumstances.

Triggers

Think about what triggers the Dog's aggression and how easily these triggers are to avoid. If he only becomes aggressive if strangers act too familiar with him, then it may be easy to avoid these situations.

Aggression towards people

All dog owners need to be confident that their family, friends and visitors are safe from their dogs. If you have any fear that your dog may attack a person, then you should take all steps necessary to prevent this from happening. This may mean keeping your dog isolated from people by securing him on a leash, or keeping him outside when you have visitors in your home.

If your dog develops aggression towards people as he gets older, then it may be as a result of a medical condition. Speak to your vet to try to identify what might be the cause of his frustration and anger. If your dog's aggression is particularly bad and you are not feeling confident around him, then you might wish to seek advice from a professional dog behaviour expert. Someone with more experience in this field will be able to help you to understand what your canine companion is going through and suggest possible behaviour management techniques to help you deal with his aggression. *On-lead aggression* On-lead aggression, also known as leash reactivity, is a very confusing and frustrating behaviour because it is usually involves a Dog who is normally calm and friendly turning into a cranky and aggressive terror as soon as he is on a lead.

The dog's owners are usually puzzled as to how the nature of their beloved pet can change so much as a result of something so menial. When you think of it from the dog's point of view however, it makes more sense.

The lead is like a trap for him and so he is unable to investigate other dogs or people closely to work out whether they are a friend or foe. Without being able to make this assessment, the dog assumes the worst, and decides that he has to protect himself and his owner from potential threats. This is why he assumes an aggressive persona.

Possible solutions to this problem are:
- to walk at less busy times if possible,
- cross the road or turn around when you see another dog approaching
- ask your vet or pet store about different types of halters and leads that are specifically designed for on-lead aggression.

How to avoid being attacked

As a dog owner, you will probably be spending a fair amount of time around your own dog and other dogs. Visiting the park, walking, or even when visiting friends with dogs all present the possibility of being attacked. It may also be that the Dog you have welcomed into your home has come from a rescue shelter and you may not have a complete understanding of his history. In any case, it is a good idea that you know how to avoid being attacked, or how to best handle yourself if an attack occurs.

The first rule to remember if you are confronted with an aggressive dog is to try to remain calm. Although this may be difficult in the situation, it is true that animals can sense fear and that this gives them more confidence in their own actions. Getting stressed or screaming may also make you appear more threatening which can provoke the dog further.

Secondly, you want to think about your body language. Don't run away as this draws on the dog's predatory nature and encourages him to chase and attack you. Instead stand completely still and avoid eye contact as he will see this as a challenge.

Ignoring the dog and not responding to the aggression in any way increases the chances that he will simply lose interest in you and walk away. If the threat continues, offer the dog something else to bite or chew on, such as a bag or drink bottle. If he gets distracted by something else, then you will hopefully be able to move away slowly.

Walking Your Cocker Spaniel Dog

Walking your Dog is an essential way for it to get the exercise and stimulation he needs for an active and healthy life. It is particularly important if the dog is regularly confined in a small space with little opportunity for exercise. Walking your pet is also a great way to assist it with socialising and dealing with the rest of the world.

For all its benefits, dog walking can be extremely frustrating, painful and even dangerous if your dog doesn't behave the way you'd like him to whilst on the lead. Many Dogs become excited, boisterous and distracted while out for walks and this can make it a very stressful experience for the walker.

Why do Cocker Spaniel Dogs pull?

The important thing to understand is that it is not a natural feeling for a dog to be constrained by a leash. Your Dog wants to run and explore the exciting world, to sniff every tree, to chase every butterfly and to urinate on as many blades of grass as possible. In his mind, there is a lot to accomplish on the short time that he's out of the family home, yard or garden, and he mustn't waste a minute. Unfortunately, for your four-legged friend, the world is not necessarily the safest place for him to go tearing about unrestrained. And for him to get the exercise he needs, it has to happen in a controlled and safe manner.

That's why it's so important that you establish good walking behaviour with your dog as soon as possible. It's a good idea for you and your Dog to attend training classes together as the instructors will be able to give you helpful hints and guidance in learning to walk together in a safe, comfortable and relaxed manner. Ask your vet or pet store about dog behaviour classes in your local area.

If you're unable to attend a training class, then you will have to train your Dog to walk properly on your own. It's important that you walk your dog at least once a day, and that you are consistent in your approach to training so that he learns the right way to behave. Maintaining a fast pace on your walks reduces the opportunities for your dog to get distracted by interesting smells you might pass along the way.

You might find it useful to tire your dog out a bit before taking him for a walk. Playing a game of fetch, or taking him to an off-leash area for a run, might make him less keen and energetic for your walk which will then make him pull less.

Discipline

Silent correction

Disciplining your Dog doesn't mean that you yell and scream at him when he does the wrong thing. In fact, this type of response can actually have a negative impact by confusing the dog, making him scared and potentially aggressive, not to mention being very stressful and negative for you.

The main objective of discipline is to have your dog understand what actions are unacceptable, and have him refrain from doing certain things that you don't approve of.

A more effective discipline strategy is "silent correction". This method is based on you remaining calm and quiet, and thereby encouraging your dog to mimic this behaviour. It is a much more peaceful, and ultimately more effective, method of disciplining your pet.

There are 4 levels of silent correction that you can use in different situations with your Dog. The appropriate level will depend upon the type of unacceptable behaviour that he is engaging in.

Level 1 –Turn away

If your Dog is persistently nudging at you, jumping up on you, rubbing against you, or demanding your attention in some other way, then simply turning your face away from him should be sufficient to indicate that you are not interested in his demands and that he won't be rewarded with your attention by behaving in that manner. If he is jumping on you, then you may need to stand up and turn your whole body away from him. Don't say anything or touch him. The key is not giving him any recognition at all for behaving in this unacceptable way.

When he has calmed down and walked away from you, take some time and then, when you're ready, call him to you an give him a pat and a treat. This will help him to recognise that he needs to respect your space, but that you still love him and will give him affection at a time that suits you.

Level 2 – Guide and hold away

If you have tried the "turn away" response mentioned above and your Dog hasn't taken the hint and is persisting in trying to get your attention, then you will need to be more assertive.

It's important that you don't respond emotionally (even if you are getting annoyed), that you don't speak to your dog, and that you don't make eye contact. All of these actions send mixed messages to your dog as they show him that he has got your attention and that he has therefore succeeded in his mission.

Instead, you need to remain calm and firmly guide the dog away from you. Hold him by the collar at an arm's length distance from you until he has relaxed and then let him go. If he comes back to you, then simply repeat the "guide and hold away" motion until he has stopped. If he continues to bother you, then level 3 may be required.

Level 3 – Guide and walk away
This response can be used in a variety of situations where your Dog is doing something that you don't want him to do. For example, if he is persistently jumping up on you or a guest, or if he is climbing on furniture.

As soon as you see him doing something that you find unacceptable, then you need to intervene so that he knows that behaviour is not allowed. You also need to be consistent in enforcing these rules so that your dog gets a clear message about what he can and can't do.

Again, with level 3, you should remain calm, silent and refrain from making eye contact with your Dog. You need to quietly walk to your dog, take him by the collar, turn him around 180 degrees from the area that he was interested in (whether it be a person, piece of furniture or something else) and walk him away.

If convenient, you may choose to take him to his bed, but any quiet spot away from the area of interest will do. Hold him there for a few seconds until he relaxes and then walk away. You may need to repeat this several times until the offending behaviour ceases.

Level 4 – Time Out
This final level can be used if the previous 3 levels haven't worked, or if your dog has done something that is completely unacceptable, such as biting or jumping on children. The objective here is showing your dog that if he does these things he will be left alone.

If practical, then you and your guests should walk out of the room you're in and close the door behind you leaving himon his own. Leave him for about 15 seconds, and then walk back in. Once you're ready, call him to you and acknowledge him, only if he comes to you on your terms.

If he jumps on you or your guests when you re-enter the room, then walk out again and double the amount of time that you leave him alone for. Keep doing this until he calms down.

Remember, that the key to the silent correction method of discipline is to remain calm and unemotional without speaking to or looking at your dog. The bad behaviour that he's doing (particularly if it's jumping up on people) is to get attention from you, and by giving him attention you are teaching him that that behaviour is acceptable.

When he understands that changing his behaviour gets a reward from you then you will have a dog with much better manners.

Play

Sit and lie down

Learning to sit on command is usually one of the first skills that an owner teaches a dog. It is an important tool for behaviour and control issues, and it is a relatively easy trick for the dog to learn.

Lying on command can help you to assert control over your dog as he is unable to do all manner of naughty things (jumping up, chasing things, begging at the table or running out the door) if he is lying down. It is a good way of controlling his impulsive nature which can help to protect him and others.

It's a good idea to teach your dog to sit first, as the process for teaching lying down begins in the sit position.

Teaching your Dog to sit

Step 1
Stand in front of your dog and say "sit" in a loud and clear voice. Hold a treat in your hand about an inch away from your dog's noise.
Step 2
Slowly move your hand and the treat up towards the top of your dog's

head. When this happens your dog will usually follow the treat with his eyes and then his nose. This movement will cause his rear to go to the ground and into a sitting position.

Step 3

Once she is sitting, say "Yes!" and give the treat. Repeat these 3 steps several times.

Step 4

The next step is to get your dog to sit without the lure of the treat in your guiding hand. Leave the treat in your pocket and follow the first 3 steps outlined above with just your empty hand guiding your dog's movement. When he sits, give him the treat from your pocket as a reward.

Step 5

Next, you want to remove the hand signal. You can do this by gradually reducing the amount of movement you make with your hand. Start by holding your hand around 10 inches or so from your dog's face when saying "sit". He will probably be sufficiently accustomed with the verbal command and the anticipated reward that he will sit immediately, but if he doesn't then make a small movement with your hand over his head. This should be the prompt needed for him to drop to sitting. As before, continue to give him a treat whenever he sits on command.

Teaching your Dog to lie down

Step 1

Ask your dog to "sit". Once he is in the sitting position, give the command "down".

Step 2

Holding a treat between your fingers in front of your dog's nose, slowly lower your hand down towards the floor, between your dog's front legs. This will encourage your dog to bring his head down to the floor. When your hand is touching the floor between your dog's front paws, slowly move it in a straight line away from your dog. This will encourage your dog to bend his elbows and drop into the lying position.

Step 3
Once he is lying down, say "Yes!" and give him the treat. Move away and encourage him to get up out of the lying position. Repeat these steps about 15 times over several days until your dog seems comfortable with this new skill.

Step 4
The next step involves using a simple hand gesture, without a treat, to lure your dog into the lying position. Once again, start with your dog in the "sit" position and then say "down". Lower your hand (without a treat) towards then ground in the same motion that you used previously to guide your dog's head and body to the ground.

When your dog is lying on the ground say "yes!" and give him a treat as a reward. Repeat this regularly for a couple of weeks until your dog begins lying down as soon as you use the cue and hand signal.

Step 5
Gradually reduce the hand signal into a small and then smaller movement. Eventually you want to simply be giving the command "down" while pointing at a position on the floor.

Step 6
The real usefulness of this command is being able to get your dog to lie down to prevent him from misbehaving or getting into a dangerous situation. For example, when guests arrive at your house, having your dog lie down on command can prevent him from jumping up and annoying or injuring them. Therefore, the next step in your dog's lying down training is teaching him to lie down when there are distractions.

The trick here is to introduce the distractions gradually. Don't start off by expecting him to lie down on command when someone knocks at the door, or when another dog comes running up to him. These are exciting situations for him and expecting him to respond to his training immediately in these situations is setting him up to fail. Start by simply varying the times and locations of your training sessions. Try each room in your house, different places in your yard and different times of the day. Then introduce gradual distractions, such as busier places in your home where family members are walking about and talking, or while you're on a walk or at the park. Then try using the command when people knock on your door or ring your doorbell.

Continuing to use treats as a reward is a good idea, but you might want to gradually phase these out as you probably won't have treats on hand every time you want your dog to respond to your commands. Using another type of reward for good behaviour, such as a cuddle, game or walk, can be an effective substitute.

Fetch

Playing fetch is a classic way of interacting with your dog. It is also a great form of stimulation and exercise that many dogs really enjoy. Some dogs get so much enjoyment from this simple game that you may find it hard to bring the game to an end! There are many different items that you can play fetch with, such as a tennis ball, a frisbee, a stick, a toy or some other specifically designed dog ball. Experiment with different items to see if your dog has a preference. Make sure that the item isn't small enough for your dog to swallow, or too hard that it might chip your dog's teeth.

If your dog doesn't seem to understand the concept of chasing after and retrieving an item, there are some simple steps that you can take to introduce him to this game. If your dog likes playing tug-of-war then start with this game and once you've worked the toy out of his mouth toss it a short distance away from you. If he runs to get it, then you immediately grab it too and start playing tug-of war again. Gradually start throwing the toy further away from you until your dog has to run for it. Encourage him to bring it back to you by playing a quick game of tug-of-war with him each time he returns. Some dogs will be really keen to chase after a toy, but they don't seem interested in returning it to you. A good response to these situations is the "bait and switch" technique. For this to work, you will need to have two identical toys to use. When your dog is excited and ready to play, show him one of the toys, throw it for him and encourage him to fetch it using a "go get it" or similar type of command.

He'll probably run after the toy, pick it up, and then look back to see what you're doing next. At that point, show him the second toy and pretend to throw it away from your dog. This will probably cause your dog to drop the first toy and come running towards you to chase after the second toy. Throw the second toy for him and while he's chasing after it go and get the first toy. Repeat this sequence for a week or 2.

This will get your dog used to chasing a toy, picking it up and then running back to you. Once this has been mastered, you can then try to phase out the second toy. Throw the first toy as before, and then call your dog once he's picked it up.

Don't show him the second toy. Hopefully, he will keep the first toy in his mouth when he comes running back to you. When he's close to you show him the second toy and at the same time say "drop it". Seeing the second toy should make him drop the first toy. Throw the second toy for him and repeat. Gradually, he should learn the meaning of "drop it" and then you can phase out the second toy altogether.

Common Behavioural Problems

Separation Anxiety

Once you have formed a strong bond with your Dog, you may find that he becomes extremely upset or distressed when you leave him alone. This is known as separation anxiety.

When a dog has separation anxiety he may engage in the following behaviours:
- Urinating or defecating where he shouldn't
- Persistent barking or howling
- Chewing, scratching and otherwise destroying household objects
- Trying to escape from his confined space
- Pacing back and forth or in a circular motion
- Eating excrement

If your dog engages in these behaviours when you're nearby, then it is unrelated to separation anxiety and you will need to take steps to control this bad behaviour. If he is doing these things while he is alone, then it may be due to separation anxiety. Separation anxiety is typically triggered by a change in the dog's living arrangements. For example, if he is given up to a shelter and then adopted by a family he may be more likely to have separation anxiety. Or, if you have previously spent a lot of time with your dog during the day, and then you suddenly get a job that requires you to be out of the house for long hours, then the change in your schedule may trigger separation anxiety. If possible, start by only leaving your dog for short periods of time and then gradually increase the duration of your absence as your dog gets accustomed to being on his own.

There are a variety of puzzles and toys designed to keep dogs occupied and stimulated while they're on their own. Some of these toys release treats periodically the more the dog plays with it. These can be a great way of keeping your dog entertained while you're out. It's a good idea to take these toys off your dog when you get home so that he gets excited to play with them again the next time you leave. Make sure that your dog gets a lot of exercise. Vary the type and location of physical activity that you engage in with your dog as this will make it more interesting for him. Keeping his mind and body stimulated will make for an overall much happier dog, which may result in less anxiety. You might also find that exercising your dog immediately before you're due to leave him on his own will help him to rest and relax while you're away.

Mouthing

"Mouthing" refers to the way a puppy, or sometimes an older dog, chews on or closes its jaws around part of a person's body. As a puppy, mouthing begins as little nips and nibbles, but as the dog gets older and his jaws get stronger this can turn into a serious bite. It's important that you establish early on with a new puppy that mouthing is unacceptable. If a puppy (under 16 weeks of age) mouths you, then you should show that you are unhappy with this behaviour by yelling "Ow!" and walking away from him.

Smiling dogs

Bearing their teeth is generally an indication of fear and aggression in dogs, however, some dogs have actually learned to show their teeth in a smile. They have seen their human companions making this type of face when happy, and they have learned to copy the expression. Of course, doing this usually provokes a positive response from the people around them, so the dog continues doing it. It's a cute, although somewhat strange, way that our dogs are trying to please us. It's nothing to worry about!

Barging through doorways

Some dogs seem to have a natural instinct to barge through a door as soon as it's opened. There are many reasons why your dog may want to do this, including:
- a desire to explore the outside world
- looking for a mate (if they haven't been neutered)

- fear of something inside.

Barging through doorways is a behaviour that should be eliminated as quickly as possible because it is unsafe for people trying to come through the door and for the dog itself. In its excitement and haste to get through the door, the dog may dart out into the path of oncoming traffic or some other threat.

The best way of dealing with this problem is by teaching your dog to sit or lie down whenever a door is opened. Instructions for teaching these commands are set out in chapter 7 of this book. If you're finding it difficult to stop this habit, then please ensure that your dog is micro-chipped or at the very least has a collar tag with your contact details on it. This will enable you to be contacted should the dog get lost or end up in an animal shelter.

Jumping up

Many Dogs like to jump up on people as a form of greeting. This can be quite a sweet display of affection as the dog is simply trying to be close to his human companion's eye level for the best opportunity to say hello. Unfortunately, because dogs can be heavy, dirty and boisterous, many people don't appreciate being jumped on by a dog.

The important thing to remember when trying to eliminate this type of behaviour is not to reward your dog with the attention that he is looking for. You need to make him understand that the appropriate way to greet a human is with all four of his feet on the ground. This means that if your dog jumps up on you when you enter the room, the best course of action is simply to ignore him.

Don't look at him, touch him or speak to him. When he realises that jumping up isn't going to get him the attention that he is craving, his feet will return to the floor. This is when you should shower him with love and affection to reinforce the notion that not jumping is the behaviour you're looking for.

On-lead pulling

Walking on a lead is not a natural situation for a dog; it's something that they need to be taught. Optimal lead behaviour has the dog walking beside its owner, not pulling ahead or trying to run off, and not lagging behind and stopping to sniff every pole and tree it passes. Teaching good walking manners takes a lot of time and dedication.

Chasing other animals

Some dogs seem to have a natural instinct to chase other animals, whether it be out of curiosity, excitement, or a more predatory desire. This behaviour needs to be strongly discouraged as it is potentially harmful for both the dog and for the animal being chased. If your dog is wildly pursuing another animal, then it may be distracted from other threats to its safety, such as traffic. Also, the other animal may scratch or bite your dog leading to injury or infection.

If your dog has a tendency to chase domestic or wild animals, then it is your responsibility to make sure that he is securely contained inside your house or garden, or that he is on a lead when you take him outside your property. You should also train your dog to come to you when he is called so that you are able to exert some level of control over him should he escape from your home or lead.

Marking

Urine marking is common behaviour for both male and female dogs. Dogs do this when they smell another dog's urine in their regular environment, which includes any place that he frequently visits. It is a way that they can communicate information about themselves to other dogs who sniff the urine. Dogs who haven't been spayed or neutered tend to urine mark more than those who have been.

Avoiding play

It's important to understand that, like humans, Dogs each have their own unique personalities. Some may be extremely playful, energetic and excitable. Others may be more relaxed, laid-back and lazy. While you can encourage your dog to play with you as much as you like, some dogs just may not be that interested in playing.

If your dog is avoiding play, there are a few things that you should consider. Possibly he is getting old. Dogs start to lose some of their energy and become less interested in play as they age. Consider whether there is possibly something medically wrong with your dog. Are they healthy and happy? A visit to the vet may be required to rule out any medical conditions. Does your dog have enough stimulation and interest? Provide your dog with plenty of toys, exercise and opportunities for play.

Tail chasing

Tail chasing may seem like a funny and harmless activity at first, but if it's encouraged it can turn into a compulsive disorder resulting in exhaustion or injury. A small amount of tail chasing is fine for puppies as they are discovering the parameters of their own body and how they are able to move.

However, if your dog continues to chase its tail a lot into adulthood, then you should take steps to reduce this behaviour. Firstly, make sure that your dog is getting a sufficient amount of exercise. He may be chasing his tail out of boredom or to burn off excess energy. Exercising him more may solve the problem by leaving him too tired and relaxed to bother with his tail. Providing him with chew-toys and other entertainment will also serve as a distraction from chasing his tail.

Digging up the garden

There are many reasons why your dog may seem determined to dig up your garden. He may be trying to create a cool and comfortable place to rest. He may want to bury a treasured item, such as a bone or toy. Or he may simply be doing it because he finds it fun. Whatever the reason for his digging, this can be a very annoying habit, especially if you are a keen gardener and like to have your garden a particular way.

Your strategy for stopping the digging is determined by the reason why your dog is digging in the first place. Maybe your dog is too warm or too cold, and he needs a more comfortable place to rest during the day.

Allowing him to stay inside during extreme weather, or providing him with shade, shelter or a comfortable bed, may make a difference. If your dog is burying items then try not to give him treats that he won't finish completely in one go. Or, if he doesn't finish a bone or a chew toy, try to get it off him once he's finished with it and then give it back to him again later. Just don't leave it with him.

A dog who digs for fun presents a more difficult problem and it may not be possible to eliminate this behaviour completely. Instead you should direct your energy into trying to minimise the damage caused by the digging. Fence off any particular areas of your yard or garden that you'd like to protect. You may also wish to provide your dog with a digging pit and encourage him to dig in this area only.

Noise Anxiety

Your Dog may demonstrate that he's afraid of noises by displaying some or all of the following symptoms – panting and drooling, whining, avoidance or attempting to run away or escape in response to a loud or unusual noise. A dog may also 'learn' to be afraid of a particular noise, for instance, if it is associated with a painful or scary experience. For instance, if a dog's tail is caught in a slamming door, then he may develop a fear of the sound of slamming doors in the future.

As with other phobias in dogs and humans, there are different levels of seriousness and whether you choose to do anything about your dog's noise anxiety should depend upon whether you see it as being detrimental to his well-being or quality of life. In less serious instances, simply avoiding the sound as much as possible and then comforting your dog when the noise occurs may be the most practical response.

If your dog's noise anxiety is more extreme then further treatment may be required. You may find that distraction or comfort may be sufficient, for example, if your dog is scared of storms then playing a game or cuddling with him during a storm may be enough to calm him down. However, remember that attempting to reassure the dog with a cuddle can have the opposite effect and make your dog think that there is actually something to be scared about.

If your dog gets really distressed, then it is a good idea to speak to your vet about possible solutions to this problem.

Bottom shuffling

It can be quite an awkward and embarrassing sight to see your be-loved Dog dragging its bottom across the carpet or grass, however there are several reasons why your dog might be doing this, and it's not a laughing matter. Bottom shuffling usually occurs because there is a source of irritation or pain in that region, and your dog is trying to find relief. You can help by taking your dog to the vet to identify and treat the source of the problem.

The most likely causes of irritation causing bottom shuffling are:

Problems with the anal glands. The anal glands are located on either side of the dog's anus and sometimes these glands can become blocked, inflamed or abscessed. If your dog has a problem with his anal glands then he may be finding it difficult to defecate, he may try to bite or lick the area, it may be swollen and he may be bottom shuffling. Your vet can easily treat anal gland issues either by prescribing antibiotics if there is an infection, by expressing the glands (squeezing out the contents if they're too full), or recommending a change in diet.

Worms. dogs with tapeworms will also bottom shuffle to try to

190

relieve the itchiness of the worms. If this is the cause of the shuffling then the worms will also be visible around your dog's anus.

The best cause of action when it comes to worms is prevention, and you should speak to your vet or dog-breeder about worm prevention medication. If your dog has worms, then your vet can administer medication to treat it.

Faecal contamination. Diarrhoea and constipation can both cause the hair around your dog's bottom to become dirty and matted. This can lead to discomfort which your dog responds to by bottom shuffling.

This situation is easily treated by washing the area and trimming away any matted hair. Make sure to check whether the skin his become infected. If so, you should seek treatment from your vet. If your dog is constipated or has diarrhoea for more than a day or 2, then you should also visit your vet.

Eating faeces

As disgusting as it sounds to us, eating their own or another animal's faeces is a normal behaviour for dogs. This behaviour is known as coprophagia, and although it is most common in puppies and nursing mothers, it can occur in other adult dogs. There is little explanation for this strange behaviour, although if the dog is an impoverished environment lacking in nutritional food or a sufficient amount of food, then coprophagia is likely to be more common.

If you want to stop your dog from eating faeces then some things to try include:
- ruling out any dietary deficiencies. Your vet may be able to assist with this if you're not sure what you're looking for.
- be vigilant with cleaning your yard and your cat's litter tray (if applicable) of faeces as soon as you're able to.
- train your dog using a "leave it" cue and reward system.

Mounting is a normal dog behaviour that is often hard to avoid. You may find your Dog mounting and thrusting up against a toy, a chair, another animal or even a person. Puppies learn to do this as they reach sexual maturity and then dogs continue doing it because they have learned that it feels good. It will typically happen when they get so excited in response to play, either with another dog or a person, that they are unable to control themselves.

If your dog's mounting behaviour isn't too often (no more than once or twice a day) and it's not bothering you, then there's no reason to try to stop this behaviour. If, however, your dog is mounting excessively, or the mounting has the potential to harm another person or animal (for instance, a large dog trying to mount a small child), then you should take steps to reduce or eliminate this behaviour.

It's also worth noting that some dogs don't appreciate being mounted, and your dog may find himself in trouble if he mounts an aggressive dog who doesn't like it. Teaching your dog to leave other dogs alone may be necessary for his own safety.

If your Dog hasn't yet been neutered or spayed, then doing so will usually reduce his or her mounting behaviour. It may not eliminate the problem entirely though. You will often be able to tell when your dog is about to mount something or someone by a change in his behaviour.

Panting, licking, prancing and pawing the object are typical signals that the dog is feeling amorous and is about to mount. Being on the lookout for these signals means that you will usually be able to distract your dog (with a toy, a game or a trained command like 'sit') before the mounting happens.

Children

Keeping your child safe

Bringing a dog home can be a very anxious experience for parents. While having a pet is a great experience for children, and one which teaches them a lot about responsibility and companionship, there is no hiding the fact that pets can be unpredictable and it's possible that your dog might be dangerous. You need to carefully monitor and continuously reassess whether or not your children are safe around your dog.

A big part of this is ensuring that your child treats your dog kindly and respectfully. Young children should always be supervised around animals as they may unintentionally frighten or be too rough with your dog. If you're unable to supervise your dog and child, then they should be separated.

When a Cocker Spaniel is hurt or startled, he may respond with a growl or a snap. This can be frightening for the child and parent, however, it is usually just the dog trying to establishhis own boundaries. Many dogs will tolerate an amazing amount from a child, but there are some limits.

At the same time, the child needs to be taught the right way to treat an animal. You should also teach your child that, even if her pet dog at home is kind and loving and patient with her at all times, not all dogs are as reliable. Kids need to understand that they shouldn't approach and pat dogs that they don't know in the park or street without the owner's permission.

Another potential problem with dogs and kids are the dogs who love kids but are too large or high spirited to play with them appropriately. These types of dogs need to be trained not to ever jump up on people. Teaching your dog to sit or lie down on command can be effective ways of calming him down when there are children around.

Health and Happiness

Grooming

Grooming is very important for your Cocker Spaniel's health and well-being. Grooming is also a good time for you to demonstrate your love and affection for your dog, which will encourage the bond between you to grow and develop. There are many professional pet grooming services available these days, and vets will also often offer grooming treatments, if you don't have the time to do it yourself.

Grooming is essential for all types of dog, regardless of their age, size, sex and breed. It is important that you set aside some time on a regular basis to make sure that your dog receives the grooming that she needs and deserves.

There are many different elements involved in making sure that your dog is well groomed.

The factors that you need to consider include:

Eyes and ears

It's important that your dog's eyes and ears are kept clean in order to prevent irritations and infections.

Examine your dog's eyes and ears on a regular basis, paying particular attention to any signs of inflammation, redness, unusual smells, or discharge. You can wipe discharge away from your dog's eyes using a clean, damp cloth.

You shouldn't try to clean out your dog's ears unless you have discussed with your vet or dog groomer the best technique and which products you should use. Attempting to clean your dog's ears if you don't know what you're doing can cause irreparable and painful damage.

You dog may be telling you that there is a problem with his eyes or ears if he is shaking his head a lot or attempting to rub his face or head with his paws repeatedly. If your dog is doing this a lot and you're not sure why, then you should visit your vet for assistance.

Teeth

Like other animals, dogs are susceptible to periodontal diseases. In extreme cases the teeth may rot, become infected and either fall out or need to be extracted. This can be a painful and distressing experience for your dog, as well as making future eating and comfort difficult.

One way of reducing your dog's risk of teeth problems is to regularly brush her teeth. Most pet stores or vets sell special dog tooth brushes and toothpaste and it is recommended that you use these on your dog around two or three times a week for maximum oral hygiene.

Obviously, it may seem quite unusual and strange for a dog to have his teeth brushed. If he doesn't like it, then it may be more effective for you to use a piece of clean cloth instead of a toothbrush. Wrap the material around your finger and gently rub the surfaces of your dog's teeth and gums.

Another way of caring for your dog's teeth is to provide him with chew toys, bones and other edible chewy items that are designed to strengthen and clean the teeth. Your vet can advise you on the most suitable chewy treats and toys for your dog.

Nails

Trimming your dog's nails can be a daunting experience for you and your dog. Cutting the nails too short can be very painful for your dog and traumatic for you as no-one wants to inflict that level of distress upon their pet. It is however, important that your dog's nails are kept at a manageable length. If they get too long they can break which may lead to infection and pain. Long nails can also change the shape of your dog's toes which can cause problems for your dog's gait and skeletal structure.

If you are concerned about trimming your dog's nails, then you may prefer to have a professional dog groomer or vet assistant do it for you.

Massage

Massaging your dog serves two important purposes. Firstly, it can help your dog to relax, particularly when he is stressed, and will reinforce that you are a source of peace, comfort and security for him. Secondly, massage can help you to monitor your dog's health and well-being. Running your hands over his body gives you the opportunity to identify whether he has any injuries, lumps, parasites or other causes of concern. Identifying these potential health threats earlier can prevent them from becoming more serious than they need to be.

Castration

Unless you intend to breed from your male Cocker Spaniel, castration is highly recommended. Besides preventing the number of unwanted puppies that are uncared for and tragically have to be euthanised, there are also a number of medical and behavioural benefits of neutering your dog.

Your dog will be safe from testicular cancer, and will have a lower risk of developing prostate cancer, if he is neutered. Castration reduces the level of testosterone in your dog's body which typically results in the following changes in his behaviour:

- Less urine marking:
- Less inclined to roam as he won't be looking for females in heat. This means that he is less likely to get lost or injured while roaming.
- Less aggressive behaviour towards other male dogs. Unneutered dogs have a natural instinct to be competitive with one another and this often fuels aggression.
- Reduced inappropriate mounting.

In order to benefit from the behavioural improvements listed above, it's best to have your dog neutered before he reaches sexual maturity. This happens between 6 and 9 months of age. You will probably still see some improvements in having your older dog neutered, but you may also need to complement this with other behaviour management techniques.

Your dog can be neutered after it reaches 8 weeks of age, although some breeders and vets recommended waiting until the dog hits puberty at around 6 months of age. It's a good idea to speak to your vet about the best time to neuter your dog and what the procedure involves.

Spaying

As with castration, spaying affords many benefits to your female dog and to the community at large. Unless you want to breed from your dog and assume responsibility for caring for or finding loving homes for the offspring that she produces, then you should have your dog spayed. It is the most responsible course of action that a dog owner can take.

The medical benefits of spaying your dog include the following:
* Reduced risks of mammary cancer and uterine infections
* Reduced risk of ovarian and uterine tumours and cancer
* Elimination of the stress and potential danger of having puppies.
* Female dogs that aren't spayed have two heat cycles per year (each lasting for a few weeks) and during these times her behaviour will usually change significantly.

After she has been spayed, you will usually see a reduction in the following undesirable behaviour:
* Less roaming
* Less frequent urination and total elimination of bloody discharge. The frequent urination while in heat is designed to attract male dogs. When she urinates less, the male dogs will have no reason to visit.
* Reduced irritability. The cycles can be painful and disturbing for your dog which can, in turn, make her fearful, nervous and irritable. Spaying relieves your dog from this discomfort.
* Less aggressive. Female dogs in heat will often fight for the attention of a male, or they will become very possessive and guarding over certain objects treating them as puppies.

As with male dogs, it's preferred that you have your female dog spayed before she reaches sexual maturity which occurs between 6 months and 1 year of age.

Training Cocker Spaniels

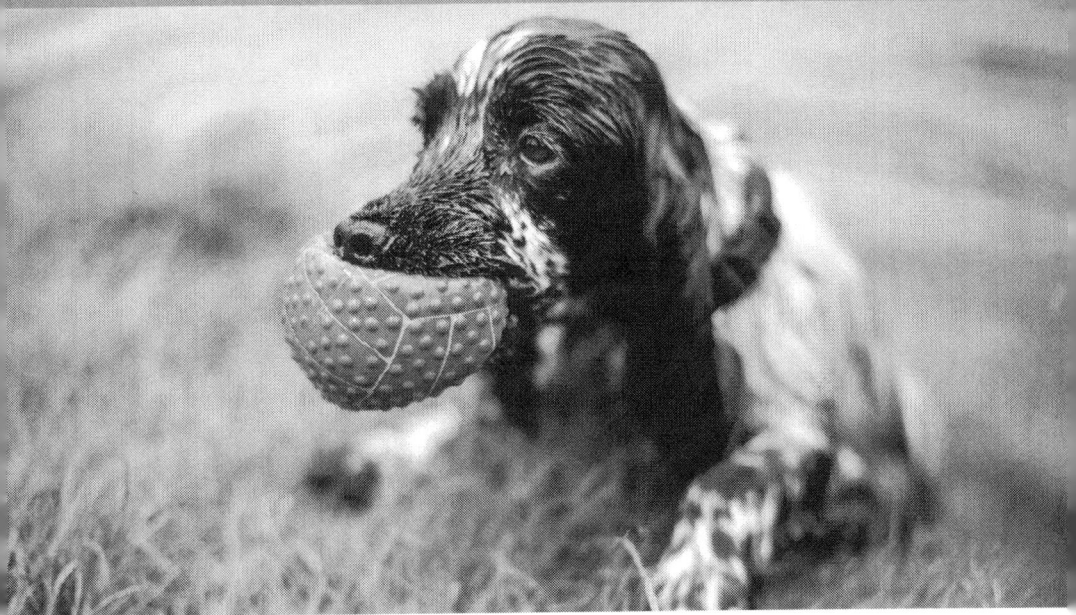

Early Puppy Training

Bringing home a new Cocker Spaniel puppy is an exciting event for the whole family. It is also exciting for your new furry friend. He needs to learn the rules of your house, though before he begins making rules by himself that may not please you.

Housebreaking

There have been many books and blogs written on housebreaking puppies, and many will have ideas that you can incorporate into a successful house-training program for your new puppy.

When you housebreak your puppy, it is essential to reward him when he goes to the toilet (eliminates) in the place you want him to, which is usually outside the house. At the same time, he must learn that doing so inside the house is not acceptable.

Crating is sometimes used in housebreaking, but it is better to keep confinement time to a minimum. Some puppies learn very easily where they can eliminate and where they cannot. Others will take longer to learn. By the time your puppy is four or five months old, he will probably be trained, and possibly well before that.

It is not unusual for a puppy to catch on for a while and then go back-wards, either. Puppies do not have excellent bladder or bowel control when they are young. Your puppy may understand that he needs to go outside, but not yet be physically capable of always controlling his growing body.

How Often Should You Take Your Puppy Out?

Cocker Spaniel puppies are all unique individuals, but most can only hold their waste for the number in hours that they are months old. Therefore, a six-month old puppy may only be able to go six hours without having a chance to go outside. He will usually be able to hold it better at night, since he is not drinking or eating and is usually inactive.

Steps in Housebreaking

1. Take your puppy outside on a schedule that is consistent. Every hour is a good starting point, and a short time after naps, playtime and meals. Your puppy will need to go out the first thing each morning, right before he goes to sleep at night and before you crate him or leave him alone in your house.
2. Maintain the same feeding times each day and do not leave food out between his meals.
3. In between the times you are taking him out, keep an eye on him. Watch for any signs that he needs to go to the bathroom, so that you can anticipate the need and help him get outside before he has an "accident". Signs your puppy may show when he needs to go out include circling, whining, sniffing, pacing or leaving the room. Take your puppy outside as soon as you can if you see one

or more of these signs. Not all puppies will learn to let you know by scratching at the door or barking when they need to eliminate. Some may pace a little and then go to the bathroom inside the house.

4. If you cannot be home to watch your puppy, you should confine him to a small room or a crate. If he has his own room that you leave him in, close the door or use a baby gate to block the exits.

5. As he becomes more housebroken, your puppy can be given more freedom, with a larger room or multiple areas within the home. After he goes to the toilet outside, allow him some free time in the house and then place him back into his small room or crate. As he becomes more consistent, the times of confinement can be shortened.

6. Go outside with your puppy and give him a reward when he eliminates outside. Praise him, take a walk with him or give him a treat. Take him to the same area every time he goes out. He will smell the "purpose" of the area and understand what you expect him to do. Your puppy may eliminate when you first take him out for a walk, but others play and move about more before they eliminate.

7. If you catch your puppy eliminating inside the house, clap twice, to startle him but not to scare him. If he stops in mid-steam, take him quickly outside. You may have to use his collar to run outside with him. If he finishes eliminating in the yard or designated area, reward him with lots of praise and perhaps a treat.

8. If your puppy does not eliminate when he does get outside, he may have been finishing up when you caught him in the act. Watch him a bit more closely when he is inside.

9. If your puppy has an accident in your house, and you find it after the fact, do not correct him. He will not connect your punishment with an accident he had hours ago, or even minutes ago.

Crate Training

You may wonder why your puppy likes to snuggle under chairs or in tight spaces. Dogs are naturally adapted to live in dens, and they look for spaces that feel like a den to them. A dog crate is an excellent den, and can give your puppy a secure and safe environment that he will not mind going to at all.

Crate training is the most effective and quickest way to housebreak puppies. Your puppy's natural instinct is to avoid his own waste, so he will try very hard not to eliminate in his crate.

Selecting a Crate

Choose a crate that has room for your puppy to stand in, and to stretch out in. If you buy one that is too big for him, he can still sleep in one end and eliminate in the other, which defeats the object of using the crate to housetrain. If you want one crate to last into his adulthood, select one with a divider panel to use when he is still small.

Place your puppy's crate in the living area during daytime hours, so he can be with you and your family, if you have one. Put his crate in your bedroom at night if possible, so that he can sleep near you, since you are part of his "pack". This gives you an opportunity to correct your puppy if he fusses while he is in the crate.

When you release your dog from his crate, take him outside right away. Encourage him to eliminate while he is out and praise him when he does. Supervise him whenever he is in the house if he is not totally housebroken yet.

Keeping Your Puppy on a Schedule

If you maintain regular feeding times with your puppy and use his crate as outlined here, you should have a puppy that is happy in his crate, when you need him to remain there.

If your puppy likes to chew things to the point of being destructive, especially when unsupervised, anxious or bored, you can use a crate when you are away for eliminating this habit. Your dog probably sleeps most of the time you are at work anyway, so crating him gives him a den, while it protects your furnishings from chewing. It also prevents your puppy from eating anything that might harm him.

If your puppy experiences separation anxiety when you are leaving home, this is because he is a pack animal. He does not deal well with isolation, and he does not know when you will return. Giving your dog a positive experience with crating helps to remedy his separation anxiety.

The crate should never be used for punishment. It should be a place where your dog enjoys spending idle time.

If you will be travelling with your dog, he will need a crate. Preparing him when he is still young gives him a positive experience and ensures less stress while travelling. When you properly train your puppy, he will not resent the crate, and it will become a sanctuary for him.

Advanced Puppy Training

How to Nip Nipping in the Bud

Even the friendliest Cocker Spaniel puppy will sometimes nip you or your family. He gets attention when he does this, and he may be teething, too. Most puppies grow out of this habit, but you do not want to use over-correction while it is still occurring.

Teach your new puppy by reacting with an "ouch" when he bites a bit too hard. As he discovers that people are sensitive to his nipping, he should respond in a positive way and stop with most of the nipping. When puppies nip, they are usually playful. Make sure your new friend has plenty of dog-safe chew toys at his disposal. Play with him only when he is being gentle with you. You may also keep a toy with you as a substitute for nipping your hand, but it cannot feel like a reward to the puppy when you substitute a toy, or he will be getting positive reinforcement instead of you asking him to change this behaviour.

Be sure your puppy gets plenty of exercise, to use up all that extra energy he has. He should also get solid rest time, at least 12 hours a day. Chew toys need to be readily available for your dog, when he wants to chew.

It is natural for dogs to chew, but you don't want your puppy wrecking expensive items in your home. Your dog may chew when you are away, too, if he is anxious because you are gone.

Lonely dogs may chew because they are bored. Give your dog plenty of exercise when you are home, so that he'll be tired and sleep more readily when you are away. You may also give him a place that is his alone, like a kennel or a crate. You can use a small room like your second bathroom, if you want to give him more room. This assumes that he is already housebroken and doesn't need a crate for that reason.

When your dog shows a love for chewing things he shouldn't, keep him crated while you are away. Give him several chew toys that are safe for him even while you are not there to supervise him. This means toys that cannot be easily consumed. Kong Toys with food or treats in them work well, but many toys come with a warning that dogs should not play with them unless they are supervised.

Don't give your puppy old towels or shoes to play with. He doesn't know the difference between old and new items, and you will be inadvertently telling him it's OK to chew on your new shoes, too.

When you leave your home, put your puppy in the area you have selected for his confinement and give him several safe chewies. Avoid long good-byes, because those may tend to make him more anxious. Just tell him that you'll see him later and head on your way.

Give your puppy as few opportunities to chew foreign objects as you can, which means confining him whenever you leave. As he becomes more predictable, you can place him in his crate with the door left open. Leave the house for 10 or 15 minutes and check for any chewed objects when you return.

If your dog seems overly anxious when you leave the house, he may have separation anxiety, which can also lead to chewing. He is a pack animal and he worries when you're gone.

Select a meat-scented bone made from nylon, which will be safe for him when you're not home. Play with your puppy and this bone a few times every day. The bone will be more interesting for him not just because of the meaty scent, but because of your scent, as well.

You can help an anxious dog to adjust the same way that you would a lonely dog, but it may take more time to accomplish the goal of not chewing on something he shouldn't. Slowly increase his alone time crated with the door open, so that he can adjust to your being out of the house, without feeling so anxious.

You are the Alpha dog

As a responsible dog owner, you need to be sure that your puppy knows his rightful place in your pack of humans. Your puppy may initially growl at humans when eating, or guard his food. You need to establish from day one that you are the alpha dog.

The puppy cannot be allowed to take your place. When your puppy knows his place in the household pack, he will be happy and better adjusted. He will not be confused or suffer as much separation anxiety, and he won't display unwanted behaviour due to not knowing where he stands in the pack.

Communicating with Your Cocker Spaniel that You Are the Pack Leader

Taking your puppy for a walk is the easiest way to let him know you are the leader of the pack, and that this pecking order will not be changed with his addition to the house. In a walk that teaches pack rule, your puppy must walk beside you or behind you.

In his mind, the pack leader is always in front. If your dog is always pulling you when you walk, he is trying to take your place as the natural pack leader.

Your puppy should be beside you or following you, rather than trying to lead you. A daily pack walk will release his pent-up energy and satisfy his migration instincts.

Feeding Time – Humans First

All the people in your house should eat before your puppy does, since the leader in a pack always has his fill before the rest. If it's time for a puppy meal but not one of your own, eat a small snack before you give him his meal. This reinforces the fact that the pack leader eats first. Do not feed your puppy table scraps while you eat a meal. Feed your dog at a consistent, scheduled time. You choose the time, not him.

Movement in the Home

If you and your puppy are going upstairs, you should go first. The same thing is true with moving from one room to another or going through doorways. You must always proceed before your dog. If your puppy does not catch on right away, have him sit and then allow him to come after you have gone past.

Greeting Guests

You should greet your guests before your dog does so. He should be the last one to get attention, in deference to humans as pack leaders. If your puppy happens to be lying down between you and wherever you are headed in the house, step over him or ask him to move. Never change your route to go around him, or you are deferring to him.

Eye Contact

If your dog tends to be dominant, eye contact will be a challenge to him. Which ever one of you averts his eyes first is the loser. It is best not to stare at your dog, since if you blink, he will think he is establishing more control.

Sleeping in Your Bed

It's not ideal for your dog to sleep with you in your bed. In his natural world, the top dog gets the best sleeping place. If you do want to let him sleep with you, invite him up and do not let him push you around as he settles in. It is best for the alpha dog training if he sleeps at the foot of the bed and not close to your pillows.

Mouthing or Biting

Your puppy must not mouth, nip or bite anyone, even when he is playing. Do not play tug-of-war with your puppy, until he is established in the pack. When you decide to let him win, he thinks this indicates that he is the top dog.

Human Emotions and Your Puppy

When you and your family are around your puppy, avoid showing emotions like nervousness, anxiety or fear. He will sense those emotions and see you as a weak leader. Think calm but big, and be consistent, assertive and calm with your puppy. Dogs can read human emotions quite easily, and you need to project your leadership whether it is spoken or not.

Caveats

You do not have to become Hitler in front of your dog. The alpha dog emotions will become more natural. You can modify the behaviour above if you feel that your place as alpha dog is fully established. Being the lead dog doesn't mean that you can't spend time snuggling with your dog. For many of us, this is why we got a dog in the first place. Just be sure that he doesn't think he is the boss.

Dogs must be taught to walk calmly on a lead. They don't instinctively know that they are not supposed to run ahead of you and play.

Teaching your puppy manners on the lead is a challenge, since they naturally move faster than we do. Your puppy is also probably excited about being outdoors. Leads constrain the natural movement and behaviour of a dog. Some dogs want to be forever running, and others want to sniff everything you walk past. If you don't want your dog to pull when he is on a lead, you must never let him pull you. If you are not consistent about this, your dog will keep pulling you on walks.

Teach Your Cocker Spaniel pup to Walk Calmly on a Lead

Dogs at dog shows and in TV ads prance beside their handlers, attentive to their desires. Dogs don't do that naturally. They had to be extensively trained in heeling. This means constant attention from you, and your puppy. Even dogs that heel are usually allowed to walk more normally on the lead when they are at home.

There are various useful methods for teaching dogs to walk on a lead without pulling. Until your puppy learns not to pull, every walk is a training session. Especially for puppies, these sessions should be short, fun and frequent.

Walking doesn't have to be the only exercise your puppy gets. He will pay more attention on a lead if you play with him first, toss a ball, and get him tired. This means he won't have as much excess energy when you take him for walks, and he will be easier to teach.

Walking without pulling can be done more easily with treats that are even tastier than the ones he probably always gets at home, just for snacks. Soft treats work well. Make sure that the treats you use are small in size, to keep your dog's mind on the training being done.

Small treats also help to avoid your dog becoming overweight - training can mean a lot of treats! Remember - if a lot of training and treats have taken place during the day, reduce their evening meal to ensure they don't get too many calories a day.

Walk at a steady, quick pace. If your puppy tends to run, he won't be able to stop and sniff everything you go past. You are actually more interesting to your dog when you are moving quickly, too.

Control Begins Before the Walking

If your puppy is going to pay attention to you and the lead while he walks, he must first pay attention before the walk begins. If he is very excited to go on a walk, focus on calming him first. Walk to your door and pick up his lead. If your dog begins dancing and barking, stand still until he calms down.

After he is done prancing, and is standing still, reach down slowly and attach the lead to his collar. If he starts dancing and jumping, take the lead off and wait until he is quiet and calm. Repeat this until your dog will wait calmly for you to attach his lead. This seems tedious when you first start doing it, but it will certainly pay off.

On the Lead

As long as you have already trained your dog to sit and to come, even when there are distractions, you can train him to walk on the lead. Walk in whatever direction you select. If the dog reaches the end of his lead and pulls, stop dead and wait until he stops pulling. Bring him back to you at this point and have him sit. After he sits, praise him. Then resume your walking.

Whenever your puppy pulls, repeat the actions above. If he stays next to you while you walk, reward him. This will help him to learn that if he stays with you, he gets praise, and if he runs ahead, he must stop. If your puppy is enticed by a smell or wishes to eliminate, make him stop and come back to you. In this case, then allow him to eliminate or sniff the curious object.

That is his reward. Follow him to the area of interest so that he doesn't pull again and disrupt the training process. Be sure to reward your dog when he walks with slack in the lead, so he will continue learning to walk without pulling you along.

Young Cocker Spaniel Training

We have spoken about some of the important commands you should teach your puppy. The information below will add to these plans, and incorporate them into basic beginner obedience training for you and your dog.

Starting Puppy Obedience at Home

Starting obedience at home gives you a place with few distractions. Your puppy is already familiar with his home, so there won't be environmental stress. When your puppy is in this learning stage, he won't have the distractions that he will have in organised obedience classes.

Your new puppy does not have a long attention span. Keep his training times short and end on a positive note, even if there have not been many of them in a session.

Building a Relationship with your Cocker Spaniel

Building a good relationship with your dog can be best done by interacting with him in accomplishing simple tasks. Playing hide and seek or teaching your dog to go over small obstacles will connect your dog with you and build his interest in you.

It's important to keep moving. Dogs play, hunt and learn while they are moving. The only time they aren't moving is when they are resting and sleeping. If you remain stationary, your dog may lose interest in working with you.

You can use treats when you are training your dog, if you like. They should be soft, so that your puppy won't spend much time eating them. It is best to keep his mind on the training at hand. Your dog should pay attention to you, not just the treats.

When your dog gives you his full attention, he is ready to begin early obedience training. Patience is the key as you work with your puppy.

"Come!" — Teaching the Recall Command

It's important to have a dog that will come immediately to you when called. When you train a puppy, you are creating his behaviour from the start, but if you adopt an adult dog, he may already have established behaviour to overcome.

Training your dog to come when called is of ultimate importance to his safety. He can also enjoy more freedom to play and run, if you know he will return to you when called. If you don't develop a trust that your dog will come to you when called, you will always be anxious when you are out with him.
Your dog can be a wonderful pet, but if he does not respond to recall commands, his training has failed him.

The training for recall command requires two people. One person will hold your dog, while you go about ten feet away from your dog and call to him enthusiastically. The first step is to involve him actively in the training. After you call to your dog, he should pull against the person holding him back. When his attention is fully on you, the other person should let him go.

As your puppy is heading towards you, take a few steps backwards and lure him further. This will make his drive to get to you even stronger. Once your dog has reached you, give him lots of praise, and back up a bit more so that he comes with you.

While you are still praising your puppy, hold his collar for a brief time and then let him resume playing with you. This will further let him know that you taking the collar doesn't mean the end of his fun.
After your dog is coming to you reliably, you can hide and call him.

Keep his interest until he is fully trained and always comes when called. You may use a whistle along with the "Come!" command initially, but phase out everything except the verbal command as he progresses.

Never repeat your command during the training process. This would teach your dog that he doesn't need to come to you right away, and that you will continue calling him. Your puppy doesn't know what "Come!" means until he associates it with the recall command.

Always lavishly reward your dog when he gets it right. If you don't continue to reward him in his early training, he will stop responding to you.

Adding Distractions

Have friends or family members stand in a circle with you and your dog, and have each one call him. Each should reward him and hold onto his collar for several seconds when he goes to them.

After he is doing well with other people, change the training location. This will add more distractions and environmental stress. Put your dog on a long training line. This will not be used to correct him, but rather as a safety measure if he decides it's time to go for a run. Leave this lead loosely on the ground, only to be used if needed.

Select a location that is not too full of distractions. A dog park or busy footpath is not the place for training. Open fields work well, possibly with background distractions like traffic noise.

The exercises will be done in the same way you originally did them. Call and then reward your dog when he comes. If he seems distract- ed, take him back to a quieter area until he has a better handle on what he needs to do.

Once your dog is ready for a busier area, have another person call to your dog, and then call him to "Come!" to you as he is headed toward the other person. Don't be surprised if he ignores you the first few times, concentrating on your helper's voice, instead. Your helper should completely ignore the dog if he comes to her.

Your dog will learn that this other caller is not fun, so he will look to you. Call him to come and reward him when he does. Soon your dog will be able to remember that strangers should be ignored and that he always needs to come to you for praise and safety.

Teaching Your Cocker Spaniel the "Down" Command

Teaching your dog "Down" is useful every day and is vital in obedience and in competition. It is a more reliable and reinforcing position than sitting, and this step cannot be omitted.

The "Down" command will be used many times outside of obedience training. Some dogs have difficulty in holding a sitting position, if distractions are challenging. It is more difficult for a dog to take off from the down position. You also have more time to correct him from the down position than from the sit position.

Submission Is Part of the Training

When your dog is in the down position, he is more relaxed and more submissive. Submission does not need to be stressful for your dog. Competition dogs learn the down position in different ways to those that you will use to teach your pet the same position.

Introducing the "Down" command for your dog may be done using a reward. To use this method, lure your dog toward a reward and position him so that he is facing you from straight on. Lower the treat-holding hand to the ground and your dog's nose will follow. His rear end may still be in the air initially, so wait until this also touches the ground before you open your hand and give him your treat.

The "Down" command will only be verbally used after you are satisfied with your dog's performance. You may teach your dog "down" from standing or sitting, but the luring is the same, and you won't reward him until he is down, front end and back end both.

Be sure to teach "Sit" and "Down" at different times. Otherwise, your dog may go straight into the down position when you ask him to sit. Reward your dog well when he performs the command properly.

Teaching the "No" Command to Your dog

Proper use of the "No" command will clear up any of your dog's possible confusion about what behaviour is acceptable and what is not. You may use the "No" command more commonly than others, once it is trained.

Your dog must understand when he is doing something that is desirable, and you will do this by rewarding him with treats or praise. He also must understand when he isn't performing properly, or using a behaviour with which we don't agree. This is what the "No" command will signal to your puppy.

Using "No" As a Non-Rewarding Signal

"No" is used to tell your dog that he is not performing the task you have asked. You must say "No" at the exact time when your dog is behaving improperly, so that he will understand why he didn't get his reward. If your communication skills are clear, your dog will learn faster.

"No" is an easy sound for your dog to recognise, and it is not usually difficult to train this command. However, make sure that he thoroughly understands "no" before you begin socialising him with other dogs.

Fun Games for Dogs

Your puppy will be a better citizen if you take the time, especially when he is young, to play games with him.

Games help in keeping your dog busy, channelling his energy into activities that are constructive, rather than activities that destroy property. Playing with your dog will deepen your relationship with him and aid in establishing you as the pack leader.

Simple Rules for Dog Play

1. Once you establish these rules, enforce them on a consistent basis.
2. Keep your games short, rewarding and interesting. Don't keep the game going after your dog has become bored. Leave him wanting more, so his head is always "in the game".
3. Take breaks when you are playing. Your dog needs time to refocus his attention on you. Frequent breaks are also helpful in keeping your dog from becoming over-excited, since he may lose control of his "play" skills and go into "fight" mode.
4. Play a variety of games with your dog, not just throwing a ball and having him get it and bring it back to you. That is a wonderful game for dogs, but they need variety, just as you do.

Playing with a Water Hose

You can use the hose to instigate a fun game of chase with your dog. Set your nozzle so that it will shoot a jet of water. Then move it around as you spray, giving your dog something to chase. He will especially enjoy this activity on hot summer days, since he does not have sweat glands in his skin. You can give your dog a bath using the hose game too, which makes it a fun activity instead of a chore.

Bathtubs often stress dogs out, and many dogs do not enjoy taking a bath. However, if your dog loves to chase water, and doesn't mind getting wet while he plays, it's a great multi-tasking tool.

Be sure you don't spray the jet of water right at your dog's face. Stop now and then and run through some of your beginner obedience training exercises, and then go back to fun. Do not let your dog jump on you during the water hose game, and don't let him try to attack the hose. If he does, stop the game and enforce your gaming rules. Not all dogs enjoy water, so this game should not be in your itinerary if your dog is not fond of chasing water or getting wet.

Play Ball

There are many games you can play with a ball that your Cocker Spaniel will probably love. Different types of ball games will have him more or less enthusiastic, so pick his favourite games to play most often.

Playing catch is a simple ball game that many dogs love. Toss a small ball to your puppy so that it can be easily caught by mouth. Be sure you choose a ball that is small enough that it fits in his mouth,but not so small that it could be accidentally swallowed.

Once your dog understands "Catch", you can make tosses that are a bit more difficult. It can also be played with a Frisbee, if you have a large enough area for play. If your puppy really loves playing catch with a Frisbee, you might train him to be a disc dog.

"Fetch" is a game that many dogs truly enjoy. It is not as easily taught as some other games, so take it slow at first. Make sure that your dog understands "Come" and "Drop" before you teach him to play fetch games.

Begin by giving your puppy a toy. After he holds it in his mouth, move several steps away and call him. Encourage him if he steps toward you and praise him when he comes all the way to you. After he is in front of you, tell him to "Drop" the toy and give him praise or treats when he gives you the toy.

Once your dog has comfortably learned the basics, throw a fetch toy just a short distance away. If your puppy ignores it, find a more interesting toy to use – perhaps one that squeaks. If your dog gets the toy and brings it to you, that is cause for big celebration and much praise. However, when learning, dogs will often run to the toy, and not bring it back. He might even grab the toy and take it somewhere else to play.

Be very patient with your puppy at this stage of game training. Every time your dog brings the toy towards you, make a big fuss over him and praise him. If he leaves the toy and comes back with nothing, offer him the toy again. After he has it in his mouth, back up a few steps and call to him, with a lot of enthusiasm in your voice. Praise him a lot if he comes toward you with the toy.

If your dog decides to run off with his toy or dares you to catch him if you can, you may need a tastier treat to help him learn. Don't chase your dog, since that rewards him for running away, which is definitely something you don't want to do. Not every dog enjoys playing fetch. If your dog doesn't think it's a fun game, choose another.

Soccer or football is a fun game to play with your dog. The idea is kicking the ball away from your dog, and getting him to chase it. Once he gets to the ball, allow him to play with it before you kick it again. You need a larger ball for soccer, and one that is difficult to puncture. Rubber balls work well. The ball should be large enough that your puppy cannot hold it in his mouth. This will make it easier for you to kick away from him, too.

Your dog might prefer chasing balls that squeak, so get him one if that pleases him in the game play. You can even dab a little peanut butter on the ball so that he will want it even more.

Socialising with other dogs

Socialising teaches your Cocker Spaniel to be a part of a larger society. Socialising puppies means aiding them in becoming comfortable as pets within our human society. Our society includes many people, noises, smells, sights – and other dogs.

Most puppies will eventually become accustomed to the things encountered in their new environment, but this is only true until a certain age is reached. Once your dog reaches that age, he will be more suspicious of new things. This is Mother Nature at work. She allows a younger puppy to become more comfortable with new things that are a part of his puppy life, so that he won't spend his whole life being frightened of non-scary things.

The suspicion developed by dogs as they age ensures that they react with healthy caution to new environmental stimuli that may be dangerous.

When Should You Socialise Your Puppy?

Your puppy will most readily accept new experiences between the ages of three and 12 weeks. After 12 weeks of age, they will become more cautious of new things. After 18 weeks, your opportunity to socialise your puppy easily will end. Every week after that makes it harder for you to encourage your puppy to accept new things.

If your puppy is well socialised, he will generally develop into a more relaxed, safer and enjoyable pet to have around. This is due to his comfort in many situations. He will be less likely to be aggressive or fearful in reaction to new situations. Relaxed dogs react in a more predictable way to everything, including vets, cats, hoovers, crowds and other new things. If your puppy is properly socialised, he will also have a peaceful, more relaxed and happier life than dogs whose environment stresses them out.

Socialisation can be done a little bit or a lot. The more new experiences he is exposed to as a young puppy, the better his chances will be of becoming a dog that is comfortable in many different situations.

Socialising your dog should be an important project for you and your puppy. Your puppy will need to be exposed to all types of animals, people, sounds, experiences and places in which you want him to be comfortable, as he grows older. Depending on where you live, this may include school playgrounds full of noisy, lively children, loud lorries, cats, crowds, crying babies or other animals. You won't be able to expose your puppy to literally everything he might see later in life, but the more he sees when he is young, the more likely he will be to be reassured in new situations.

When you socialise your puppy, don't place him in situations that overwhelm him. He should get more – not less – comfortable when exposed to the same situation again. If meeting a room full of other puppies is too much for him right now, then have just one person and their puppy come over first, and work from there.

Always watch how your puppy reacts to new situations. Be ready to lessen the stimuli if your dog becomes frightened. After every experience with socialisation, praise your dog and give him a special treat or some special time with you.

Puppy Classes

Socialising a puppy is helped by attending "nursery or kindergarten" classes for puppies. These are specifically designed for training your puppy in socialisation. Playing off-lead and pretend fighting allow puppies to meet others and play. They will learn to be gentle when they are mouthing or biting and they will become accustomed to being handled by more people. Some classes use CDs of sounds, along with props, to expose puppies to strange sounds and sights. These classes also impart a few basic obedience skills, so that makes them doubly helpful.

Obedience Training

Basic Training

We have covered some of the basics in beginner obedience training earlier in this eBook. Here is some more basic training that Cocker Spaniel should learn.

Teaching Commands

There are a few guidelines that will help in making your training easier for both you and your puppy.

1. Start with simple commands and increase the difficulty gradually: You will want to proceed step-by-step so that you're giving your puppy plenty of practice time to get the commands right. Start with the easier commands, and do them in familiar places without lots of distractions. After your dog is more predictable in his responses, and doing what you want him to do, then add distractions and distance. You will stand close to your dog when you are first training a new command. After he understands it and responds properly, take a step back, and then another, until he will perform the command without your being right next to him. Allow your dog to learn one command well before you begin another. If he doesn't perform well, remove a distraction and try the command again. Always be willing to slow down and go back to the last point at which he was performing the command response properly.
2. Be consistent in your commands: Always use the same command word for each command you are teaching your dog. If you say "Come" sometimes and "Come here" at other times, it is confusing for your dog.
3. Treats make good rewards: There are many training methods you can use, but using edible treats will allow you to lure your

dog and reward him when he responds properly. If your puppy is not interested in food, give him lots of verbal praise and perhaps one of his favourite toys. Scratching behind his ears or in another favourite spot is also a good reward.

4. Do not repeat your commands: You may do this without thinking, but it doesn't help your dog. In fact, it teaches him that he doesn't have to come the first time he is called.

5. Be patient: Yelling or jerking your dog's lead will not teach him how to come or to sit. Instead, it will teach him that you are unpredictable and loud, and that training is not a fun thing. When you feel yourself growing impatient, return to to something he does easily and then end the training session. Your dog will respect and obey you if you are calm, consistent and fair.

6. Phase out your rewards: Your dog may be more motivated when you reward him in ways he cannot predict. Once your dog knows the commands, only use treats if he does very well on his response. Vary the frequency, amount and type of reward and add praise and tummy rubs as you give fewer food treats. You won't always have treats with you when you need him to respond to your commands.

7. Keep training sessions short: Training is more effective when it is fun for your dog. Stop before you or your dog are bored. Keep sessions shorter rather than longer, and don't be a bossy person to your dog. Five to ten minutes is fine for a first training session, and mini trainings can be done any time of the day.

8. Add new people and new place: Give your dog his commands in different settings, once he has the idea of what you want. In this way, he will also respond properly to family members or friends who might be dog sitting for you sometime in the future.

9. Allow your dog to earn his treats: After your dog knows some commands, ask him to obey one before giving him a toy or a treat, or a scratch behind the ears. If he doesn't respond to your command, do not give him what he wants just yet. Wait a minute and try again. Then reward him when he obeys you.

10. Practice never ends: Just because your dog learns to "come" does not mean that he will remember it forever. He can lose his skills if you don't practice them regularly.

Mastering the skills of basic obedience training is important for you and your dog. They make the relationship more harmonious and will keep your puppy and you safe if there are emergencies in the future.

Training a dog takes a lot of patient work. Any dog is capable of learning the basic commands. If you have a bad day of training, don't be frustrated. Just try again when you are both in a better frame of mind. If you need help, seek out a professional trainer.

You are responsible for fully socialising and training your dog. Understand the amount of time it will take before you adopt a puppy or dog, so that he will be well trained and happy with you. Remember, having a dog should be fun. Don't take everything too seriously, and be sure that you and your dog have good times when you are training him. This will make him more receptive in future training sessions.

Things to Remember during Training

When you are first training, select an area that is not full of distractions for your Cocker Spaniel. Once the commands are mastered, you can move to areas with more distractions and feel confident that he will still respond to your commands. If you have two dogs, remember you can only train one at a time – with two dogs you won't have their total concentration, they will distract each other. Group training can come later once your dogs have learned the basics.

Use verbal praise and petting as rewards. Food treats are great, and they will entice your dog to perform properly. However, you may find yourself in situations where no treats are available, and he needs to respond to you properly without expecting food every time. Toys can also be given as a reward, especially if they are his favourite toys, but remember once again that in an emergency, you may not have toys with you to use to lure your dog.

Short leads are great for walking, but longer leads or long lines will work better for any training where you are placing distance between you and your dog. Make sure you are confident that he will come

222

when called and follow other verbal commands before you work with him without a long line attached. It can be left on the ground, only to be used if your dog decides that a nice run in the opposite direction sounds like fun.

Your training sessions should always end with a positive response from your dog. If he is having trouble learning a new command, and you've been working with him for a little while, go back to a command he knows, and reward him for executing that response correctly. This way, he'll look forward to his next training session.

Canine Good Citizen Classes

Most national Kennel Club's run Good Citizen Classes and you should contact them to find out where the classes are being run in your area.

In the US, The American Kennel Club (AKC) offers a program that rewards dogs who become good canine citizens. It began in 1989, and it rewards your dog if he has good manners, both at home and out in the city or community.

There are two parts to the Canine Good Citizen classes. They both stress that you need to be a responsible pet owner and that your dog should be a pleasure for others to be around. Any dog that passes the 10-step test for Canine Good Citizenship is eligible for a certificate issued by the AKC. In the UK, The Kennel Club runs a Good Citizen Class and these classes were started in 1982 and operate along similar lines to the US Classes.

~

The Canine Good Citizen Program Is a
Good Foundation for Training

~

The Canine Good Citizen program is a good first step for training your Cocker Spaniel. It will lay a proper foundation for any other Kennel Club activities that you might like to participate in, for example obedience, performance, agility and tracking. As you teach your dog CGC skills, you will be happy to discover the joys and benefits of successfully training your puppy.

Training enhances the bond that exists between you and your puppy. If your dog has a solid education in obedience, he will respond better to you and will be a more pleasant dog with which to live. In addition, your puppy will enjoy your company even more after training, since it strengthens the bond you have with your dog.

Often, Canine Good Citizen training will give you and your dog sessions that are stimulating intellectually, and this will help your dog in developing a higher quality of life. CGC is often just the beginning of a long life of successful training, in whatever types of events you think might be enjoyable for both of you.

The Popularity of a Kennel Club Canine Good Citizen Program

This program is one of the Kennel Clubs' training areas of rapid growth. The entry-level program gives you and your dog a good foundation for future training. Many countries have developed programmes. Animal control and police agencies use this program when they deal with dog issues in communities. Some groups that train therapy dogs also use CGC as a screening tool. In addition, some groups use the CGC program to teach children beginner dog training. Some speciality breed clubs, for single breeds only, give the Canine Good Citizen award programme at their yearly national dog shows. Members of clubs for dogs of all breeds realise that CGC is a popular event that lets everyone who competes become a winner. Vets appreciate dogs that are well trained, and there are more than a few CGC programmes in veterinary hospitals.

Even though the CGC programmes have not been in existence for a long time, they have had a positive impact in many communities. It can help you to assure yourself that your beloved dog will always be a well-respected and welcomed member of your community.

Companion dog Training

Companion dog training is an excellent way to teach your dog to be responsive to you, even in situations when emergencies arise. Working with your dog in companion dog training allows him to become better socialised, which means that he can retain knowledge more easily. As your puppy matures, he will be less likely to bite, and will be calmer around other dogs and other people.

Training in groups gives you a few advantages, even if training at home has been successful. If you and your dog are in a situation that has many distractions, you will want to know that you can still count on your dog to obey your commands without hesitation.

Certification Requirements

There are certain requirements of Companion Dog Program Dogs and their owners. They have adopted these requirements since you and your dog may encounter a wide variety of ordinary situations while meeting other dogs and owners in public settings. Trained CDP teams can work in the park system, and as such, they must behave as calm and professional teams.

Companion dogs must be able to respond calmly and instantly obey your commands, even in stressful circumstances. CDP teams may represent the areas in which they were trained. When you and your dog pass this programme, you can set a good example for other dogs and their owners.

Companion Dog Testing

Companion Dogs must pass an annual test with control and confidence. The actual test is extended from the Canine Good Citizen Program testing. It will involve you, your dog and an evaluator who has been properly trained and certified.

Your dog must be able to:

1. Walk easily on even a loose lead

This will demonstrate that you are in control of your dog. You may allow your dog to walk on either side of you, whichever you prefer. You must include an about turn, a right turn and a left turn, with one or more stops between them. Your dog will need to calmly stop at the end of this exercise, too. Your dog does not have to sit whenever you stop.

2. Accept friendly strangers

This part of the CDT test will demonstrate that your dog will allow someone he does not know to approach him in a friendly way, while the stranger speaks to you. You and the evaluator, who plays the part of the stranger, will shake hands and talk for a few minutes. Your dog must not show shyness or resentment, and cannot break his position or try to walk up and meet the stranger.

3. Have attractive grooming and appearance

This will demonstrate that your dog will allow himself to be groomed and examined, such as might be carried out by a dog groomer or vet. Your dog should allow a friend to examine and groom him. This also will demonstrate your concern, responsibility and caring for your dog. The evaluator will inspect your dog, comb or brush him and examine both front feet and his ears.

4. Sit politely while being petted

This test will show that your dog will allow a person he does not know to touch him in a friendly way while he is out with you. Your dog will sit at your side, and the evaluator will pet your dog on his body and head. He will then circle you and your dog. Your dog cannot show resentment or shyness.

5. Walk through a crowd

In this test, your dog must move politely among pedestrians, and remain under control when you are out in public places. You and your dog will walk around close to three or more people. It is acceptable for your dog to show interest in a stranger, as long as he is not over-exuberant or excessively shy. You may speak to your dog, to praise and encourage him. He should not be pulling on his lead.

6. Obey sit, down and stay

This test will demonstrate that your dog has been trained and will respond to your commands. You may use more than a few seconds to help your dog obey, and you may even use more than one command. In the "stay" phase, you will tell your dog to stay, and walk forward for 20 feet. Your dog may change positions, but must remain where he is.

7. Come when you call

Your dog should always come to you when you call him. In this test, you will walk 10 feet away from your dog, then face him and call him. You are allowed to add body language if you need it, and encouragement. You may ask your dog to wait or stay, or you can walk from him without verbal cues. The evaluator will pet your dog a bit, to provide a mild distraction.

8. Show little reaction to other dogs

This part of the test will demonstrate that your dog is polite with other dogs. You and another handler will walk toward each other, shake hands and speak, then continue on. Your dog should not have anything more than casual interest in the other dog.

9. Show minimal reaction to distraction

Your dog should be confident even when faced with common situations that may be distracting, like someone running by or dropping something. He may show a natural curiosity or interest, but he should not bark, show aggressiveness, attempt to run away, or panic.

10. Interact with animals in a park setting

Your dog should remain under control without reacting adversely to any other animals you may encounter in parks. Horses, dogs or other animals may be used to test your dog.

The rider of the horse or handler of the other animal will stop and chat with you, then continue on their way. A whole group of dogs and handlers or horses and riders will mill about, close to your dog. Your dog should only show a casual interest.

11. Be calm when separated from you and unsupervised

Your dog should keep his good manners and training when you leave him alone. The evaluator may ask if you would like him to watch your dog, and he will hold your dog's leash. Your dog will be with the evaluator for three minutes. He doesn't have to stay in the same position, but he cannot pace, whine, bark or howl, or display any emotions other than mild nervousness or agitation.

12. React calmly to emergency vehicles

Your dog should remain fully under control even when close to emergency vehicles. He should remain in position while vehicles go by quickly, with sirens and lights on. The emergency vehicle will block the trail on which you and your dog are walking.

An actor playing a "victim" will be attended to on the ground. You and your dog will walk by and you will ask if there is anything you can do to help. Your dog should remain under control and cannot shy away from the unusual sights and sounds.

228

Conclusion

In this eBook, you have learned about some important aspects of welcoming a new Cocker Spaniel into your home. You should also have a good idea about the best ways to make your dog a good companion and a welcome family member.

Take the time to enjoy hours spent training your Cocker Spaniel – a few minutes at a time, since his attention span is not very long. After you have bonded with your dog, you will be confident to take him out whenever you want.

You and your dog must be attentive when you are in public areas.

Your dog must be under your control whether he is on or off the leash. Your well-mannered dog will be a role model for all well-trained dogs.

If you attend a specific training club in your area, and you feel that it has benefited you and your dog, recommend the club when you speak to new dog owners. This will help to get them started off on the right paw, too.

We hope you enjoy becoming a Cocker Spaniel owner and all the joy and fun it brings! Don't hesitate to get in touch with your local vet if you have any questions – they are always happy to help.

Want to know more about looking after your pet?

The writer of this book, Dr. Gordon Roberts, is a veterinarian and owns a total of eight animal hospitals around the UK. He believes that the key to a healthy, happy pet is preventative care, which is only possible when pet owners take the initiative to educate themselves about their animals. As a result, Gordon has written dozens of useful reports on pet care in order to share his years of experience with discerning pet owners. As a thank you for purchasing this book, you can browse and download his specialist reports completely free of charge! You'll learn all sorts of useful information about how to spot possible health conditions early on, and how to make preventative care for your pet a priority, helping you save time and money on visits to the vet later on. To view and download these bonus reports, simply visit Gordon's website at: http://drgordonroberts.com/freereportsdownload/.

Best wishes,
Gordon

Printed in Great Britain
by Amazon